John Carroll

Project
2013

In easy steps is an imprint of In Easy Steps Limited
16 Hamilton Terrace · Holly Walk · Leamington Spa
Warwickshire · United Kingdom · CV32 4LY
www.ineasysteps.com

Notice of Liability
Every effort has been made to ensure that this book contains accurate
and current information. However, In Easy Steps Limited and the
author shall not be liable for any loss or damage suffered by readers
as a result of any information contained herein.

Trademarks
All trademarks are acknowledged as belonging to their respective
companies.

In Easy Steps Limited supports The Forest Stewardship Council (FSC),
the leading international forest certification organisation. All our titles
that are printed on Greenpeace approved FSC certified paper carry the
FSC logo.

MIX
Paper from
responsible sources
FSC www.fsc.org   FSC® C020837

Printed and bound in the United Kingdom

ISBN 978-1-84078-575-3

Contents

1 The Basics

This chapter introduces Microsoft Project 2013 and explains how it can help you manage your projects.

Introduction

Microsoft Project 2013 is the latest release of this popular project management tool. Managing projects can be a complex activity but, with the help of Project, you can plan, schedule, track and communicate on the progress of your project. Whether it is a simple, short-term project (like arranging a company event) or a more complex project (such as launching a new business), Project can help you stay in control of it.

This book covers both the Standard and Professional versions of Project. The main difference between them is that Project Professional allows you to collaborate and share information with other Project users in your organization. The detailed differences are noted throughout the book and summarized under Version Comparison (page 12).

Project Features

Project can produce some great-looking charts and diagrams to help you plan your project, but it can do a lot more besides:

- It can help you to understand, develop and manage project plans and schedules

- It can produce a critical path analysis to identify the areas where you will need to keep a close track on progress

- It can identify if you have too much work allocated to any one person

- It can schedule facilities, such as meeting rooms and equipment for you

- It can help you to understand and control project budgets and costs

- It can keep track of public holidays and team members' vacations and other commitments

- It can help you build professional-looking reports to communicate and present project information in an effective and understandable way

Project Enhancements

Project 2013 has introduced a number of new and enhanced features. These are indicated wherever they occur throughout the book. They are also summarized under What's New (page 10).

8

Project Management

Successful project management is about completing a project on time, within budget, and with the needs of the business fully met. While this is easy to say, a large percentage of projects fail. The most commonly quoted figure is around half of all projects, although, depending on how you define failure, it could be as little as 25% (total failure) or as much as 75% (failed or seriously challenged).

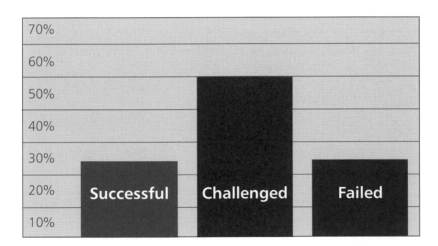

Whichever way you look at it, only around one quarter of projects end up as fully successful (i.e. completed on time, within budget, and with the required scope). In order to get most projects completed, corners have to be cut, but things still seem to take longer than expected. As a further result, costs inevitably seem to increase.

Successful Projects

It doesn't have to be that way. We know how to ensure projects are successful – it's not rocket science; it's just plain common sense. Throughout this book, you will find some basic project management concepts that have been proved in practice. Follow these concepts and advice to ensure that your project will be successful.

Microsoft Project

Microsoft Project is a great product that will help you plan, organize and control your project. It won't carry it out for you (you still have to do that yourself), but what it will do is help you to control and complete it successfully.

Hot tip

Effective Project Management **in easy steps** is a companion book and covers project management in more detail.

What's New?

With each new release of Project, Microsoft typically addresses some issues and introduce a number of enhancements. With the previous release (Project 2010), Microsoft introduced some significant changes. These included the fluent user interface (ribbon) in place of the traditional toolbars and buttons, enhanced table features (similar to Excel), user-controlled scheduling and a new timeline view.

While the changes in this release of Project 2013 are not quite so radical they do represent some enhancements and new features. These are noted, where relevant, throughout the book. But in summary the key new features and functionality are:

Updated Visuals
Along with the rest of the Microsoft Office suite of programs, Project 2013 has a new cleaner look that is designed to be simpler to understand and easier to use.

OfficeArt for Project Reports
Project 2013 now supports OfficeArt in reports. It allows you to create pictures, tables, charts, shapes and text boxes (objects) in Project reports. It also allows you to re-position, edit or remove any existing objects. This works in the same way as in Microsoft Word, Excel, PowerPoint and Outlook and consequently you can now share OfficeArt content between all these programs.

Improved Reports
With Project 2013, Microsoft has delivered a new set of report templates which use the OfficeArt infrastructure. These allow you to create dynamic reports in Project without the need to export data to another program. The feature to create data cubes for automatic export to Pivot Tables in Excel and Pivot Diagrams in Visio Professional has also been retained.

Burndown Reports
Project 2013 now supports the production of burndown charts (called burndown reports by Microsoft) which are a key requirement in agile project management methodologies. These can show planned work, completed work and remaining work as lines on a graph.

Burndown Data
In order to support the production of these new burndown

reports, Project 2013 now includes eight new fields to hold the required data:

- Cumulative work baseline (0 to 10)

- Remaining cumulative work baseline (0 to 10)

- Remaining tasks baseline (0 to 10)

- Cumulative actual work

- Remaining actual tasks

- Remaining cumulative actual work

- Remaining cumulative work

- Remaining tasks

Task Paths

This new feature allows you to highlight the entire link chain for any specific task. The link chain is the sequence of tasks that directly affect or are affected by the selected task. You can also choose to highlight predecessor or driving predecessor (critical path) tasks and successor or driven successor (critical path) tasks.

Extended Date Range

Previously, Project supported dates up to the year 2049 but with Project 2013, task and project dates are now supported up to the year 2149.

Backstage Overhaul

Microsoft now refers to what was the File menu as the Backstage view, and with Project 2013 the File menu has been revised to provide some improvements in the following areas:

- Microsoft has tried to make it somewhat simpler so that it is easier to find what you are looking for

- Project 2013 has also now been brought into line with the other Microsoft Office programs

- The File menu now provides one single location where you can open and save files in a number of different formats to your own computer or network, the World Wide Web, a Project Server or a SharePoint site

Version Comparison

There are two versions of Project 2013: Project Standard and Project Professional, together with three companion products (SharePoint Server, Project Server and Project Online).

Project Standard

Microsoft Project Standard 2013 is designed as a stand alone project planning and scheduling tool for people who do not need to collaborate and share data with other project managers.

It is offered at a reduced cost as it does not contain all of the functionality in Project Professional. As this book covers both versions, any functions that are not available in Project Standard are highlighted with warnings throughout the book.

Project Professional

Project Professional 2013 is designed to work in an environment where project managers need to share and pool information. It therefore contains some additional functionality to assist with these tasks. These are covered in detail in the book, but in summary, the two main additional features are:

Team Planner

This feature provides visual dragging and dropping of assignment changes as illustrated below:

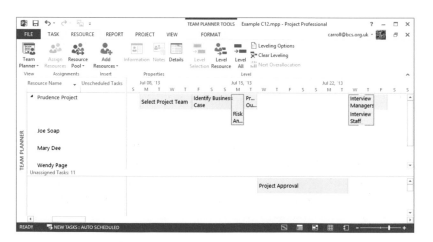

The top part of the screen displays the allocated tasks, with over-allocations highlighted in red. The lower part shows unallocated tasks. Tasks can be dragged and dropped between resources and between allocated and unallocated tasks.

Enhanced Collaboration

Integration allows project schedules to be published and shared, with SharePoint. Synchronization of schedules between Project Professional and SharePoint task lists can also be performed, so that any changes made by team members in SharePoint can be reflected back into the Project schedule.

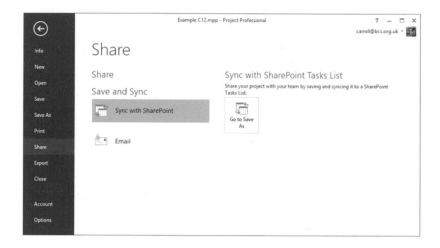

There are three main companion products available to Project Professional users:

SharePoint Server

As illustrated above, Project Professional can publish schedules to and synchronize them with SharePoint Server. SharePoint provides a simple method of organizing, synchronizing and sharing project information on smaller projects.

Project Server

Project Server provides a project portfolio management repository for all project data. It enables organizations to initiate, select, plan, and deliver projects while tracking time and budget. It also provides extensive reporting and mobile access to project data.

Project Online

Project Online (which is part of the Microsoft Office 365 product range), allows an organization to make Project Professional available from the Cloud. This allows project managers to access the latest version of Project from any PC anywhere. It also stores their settings and files so they are all available from any location.

The Gantt Chart

The first thing you see when you open or create a new project is the Gantt chart. It is the default view, and with good reason. The Gantt chart is probably the most widely used and most useful project management tool.

Summary Level

They say that every picture tells a thousand words, and this is the key picture in your project:

Please note that the dates illustrated in this book are in MM/DD/YY format.

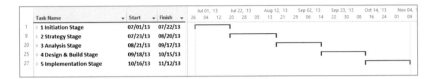

At the summary-level (as illustrated above), you can view the whole project on one screen or sheet of paper. The Gantt chart represents the most frequently-used way of representing a project graphically and is particularly useful for senior management in its rolled-up summary form (as above).

Detailed Level

At the more detailed level (as illustrated below), the Gantt chart is typically used by the project manager to communicate with the project team, and to track project progress, by task, on a day-to-day basis.

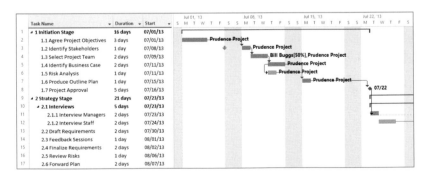

In addition to letting you view the project schedule at the strategic (high-level) and operational (detailed-level), the Gantt Chart view also allows you to insert and edit tasks, and allocate the people and other resources to work on the tasks. You can set milestones and deadlines, and generally keep track of your project and the resources working on it.

Getting Help

Getting extensive help in Project is fairly straightforward, and is only ever a couple of clicks away:

1 Click on the question mark at the top right-hand side of the Project window or press the F1 function key to open the initial help dialog box, as illustrated below

2 Click on any of the subjects under Popular searches, Getting started or Basics and beyond (for example "Critical path" under "Popular searches", as illustrated right) to open up a list of all the relevant help articles on that subject (not illustrated)

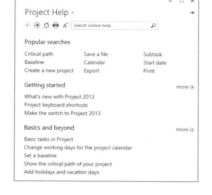

3 Click on any of the listed articles to open it up (for example, "Show the critical path of your project" has been selected in the illustration on the right)

4 If you can't see what you are looking for, click in the "Search online help" box at the top of the help dialog box and type a description of what you want help with

5 At the bottom of the list, Help also provides suggestions for other areas you can explore (as illustrated right)

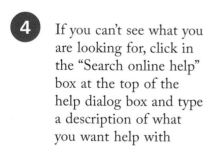

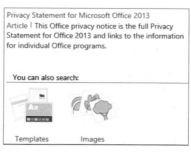

Summary

- Microsoft Project can help you to plan and schedule your project, allocate tasks, and track progress and costs

- One thing Project can't do for you is manage the actual work of your project. Around 50% of projects fail for reasons that are known and understood. This book includes some proven project management concepts to help you make sure your project is a success

- Project 2013 now features a new cleaner look, that is designed to be easier to use, in line with the rest of the Microsoft Office suite

- OfficeArt is now supported in project reports, enabling the creation and editing of pictures, tables, charts, shapes and text boxes in reports

- Project 2013 now provides a completely new set of report templates, which use the OfficeArt infrastructure, and can be used to create dynamic reports without the need to export data to another program

- The creation of data cubes is still supported, allowing the export of date to pivot tables in Excel and pivot diagrams in Visio Professional for more sophisticated reporting

- One of the more significant additions is the facility to produce burndown charts or reports, with some additional data fields to support this functionality

- Task Paths is another new feature, similar to the critical path function, that enables the highlighting of the chain of any tasks that are linked to the selected task

- Gantt Chart view is the most useful view in Project, and the one in which you will probably choose to do most of your work. At the summary level it is great for communicating strategically, while at the detailed level it is great for working with the team on a day-to-day basis

- Getting help is only a mouse-click away, or you can use the F1 key to go direct to the Project Help dialog box and full help contents

2 User Interface

The User Interface (or ribbon) replaced the old menu and button toolbars. It provides a method for accessing menu items that is compatible with the other Office applications.

User Interface

The Fluent User Interface consists of seven tabs, each of which invokes a ribbon containing different items and functions:

The seven tabs are: File, Task, Resource, Report, Project, View and Format. There is also a Quick Access Toolbar (covered on page 32) at the top left. The top center indicates the current tools being displayed (Gantt Chart Tools), together with the file name (Project1). Finally, top right are the help, window size and close functions, together with the current account user.

File

When the green File tab is selected, by clicking it, the File view is displayed. This is different from the other views tabs (as can be seen from the illustration below) and is covered on page 20.

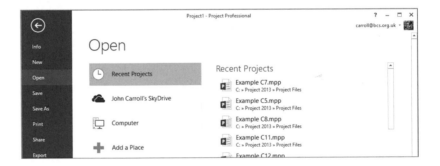

Task

This is the default ribbon in Gantt Chart view (see page 22):

Resource

Used to assign and manage resources on the project (see page 24):

Report

The Report ribbon is used to produce reports, which are covered fully in Chapter 13:

Project

The Project ribbon is used to set up basic project and status information (which is covered on page 26):

View

The View ribbon is used to control views, data, sorting and filters (which is covered on page 28):

Format

The Format ribbon is used to control the format of charts and tables (which is covered on page 30):

Unpin Ribbon

Finally at the bottom right corner of the ribbon is the Collapse the Ribbon icon (an upward chevron) which hides the ribbon, making more space in the current view. Selecting another tab brings the ribbon back into view and the icon turns into a Pin the Ribbon (pin shape) allowing the ribbon to be permanently displayed again.

Hot tip

Ctrl + F1 can also be used to toggle between hiding and displaying the ribbon.

File

When the File tab is selected, the following File view (strictly speaking it is not a ribbon) is displayed:

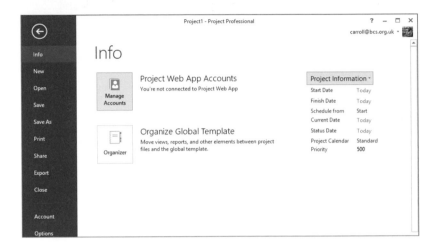

In addition to the normal File operations (New, Open, Save and Save As) down the left-hand side, there is also a further series of tabs (Info, Print, Share, Export and Close) together with Account and Options. The Info tab (as selected above) brings up the options for managing Project Web Application Accounts, Organizing the Global Template and updating the Project Information displayed.

Open

The Open tab on the left-hand side brings up a list of recently-used files and options for accessing files from other locations.

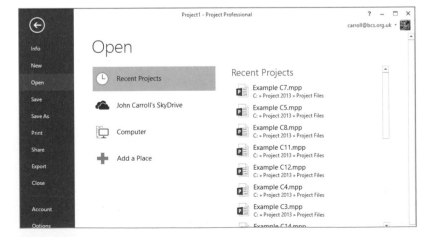

New

The New tab brings up the options for selecting a template, starting with a blank project or copying an existing project:

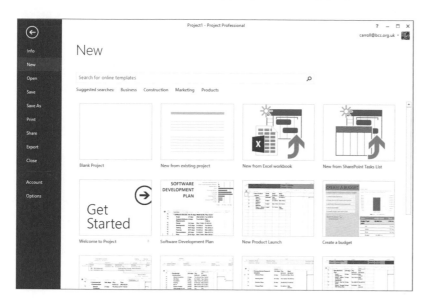

Print

The Print tab brings up the standard print options, together with a preview of what will be printed.

Share

The Share tab brings up the Save and Synchronize with SharePoint (as a project file or task list) together with the option to share by email.

Export

The Export tab brings up the options of creating a PDF or XPS document together with options for saving the project file to an earlier version of Project, as a template, as an Excel workbook, as an XML file or in some other file type.

Account

The Account tab brings up the user account, product registration information and display effects.

Options

The Options tab brings up all the detailed options for setting date, language, scheduling and other program options.

Task

When the Task tab on the user interface is selected, the following Task ribbon is displayed:

The ribbon is divided into eight groups, each containing one or more functions. Working from left to right, these are:

View

This group contains one function, Gantt Chart, which can be selected to switch back to Gantt Chart view at any time. There is also a down arrow beneath it, which produces a drop-down list of the 13 built in views (as illustrated on the right). It also has More Views at the bottom, which brings up the full list of all 27 available views.

Clipboard

This group includes the Cut, Copy, Paste and Format Painter functions. Copy includes Copy Picture and Paste includes Paste Special.

Font

This group contains the font attributes, including background color. There is also a link (at the bottom right of the group) to the Font dialog box (as illustrated on the right), where all font attributes can be set.

Schedule

This group includes the task progress functions: 0%, 25%, 50%, 75% and 100%, together with Mark on Track (which marks the task as completed up to the current date).

The group also includes functions for Indent, Outdent, Split Task, Link and Unlink tasks, Respect Links and Inactivate (to inactivate or re-activate tasks). Making a task inactive means it no longer affects the schedule or resources.

Tasks

This group contains functions to set a task to Manually or Automatically Schedule. Where a task is automatically scheduled, Project will set it to start on the current date or immediately after any predecessor tasks are completed. Where a task is manually scheduled, you will need to enter the start date and duration.

The group also contains functions to Inspect (Task Inspector provides information on scheduling details and any issues) and Move a Task. Finally, it includes a Mode function, which allows you to select whether all new tasks will be manually or automatically scheduled. Selecting this function will not change any existing tasks, but they can still be changed individually.

Insert

The Insert group contains functions to Insert Task, Insert Summary Task, Insert Milestone and Manage Deliverables (which will be grayed out unless you are linked to Project Server, a companion product).

There is also a down arrow beneath the Insert Task button that brings up further insert options, as illustrated on the right.

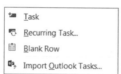

Properties

This group contains Task Information, which brings up the Task Information dialog box (as illustrated below). The group also contains Note, Details and Add to Timeline functions.

Editing

The final group includes Scroll to Task, Find (find/replace text), Clear (cell content or formatting) and Fill (a function that copies a value from one cell into one or more adjacent cells).

Resource

When the Resource tab on the user interface is selected, the following resource ribbon is displayed:

The ribbon is divided into five groups, each of which contains one or more functions. Working from left to right, the groups are:

View

This contains one function, Team Planner, to switch to that view (only available in Project Professional). There is also a down arrow beneath it, which can be selected to produce a drop-down list of the 13 built-in views and a More Views option that produces the full list of all 27 available views.

Assignments

This group contains the Assign Resources and Resource Pool functions. If Assign Resources is selected, the Assign Resources dialog box opens (as illustrated right) and displays the available resources for the project.

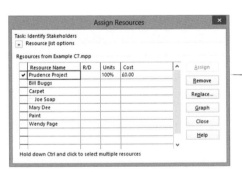

If Resource Pool is selected, a drop-down list offers: Share Resources, Refresh Resource Pool, Update Resource Pool and Enterprise Resource Pool. Share Resources opens the dialog box (as illustrated right) and allows resources to be shared over several

projects, by creating a common resource pool. This allows control of resources working on more than one project.

Insert

This group contains one function: Add Resources and, if selected, it will display the options illustrated right. Work Resource or Material Resource will allow you to add the new resource name. Alternatively, you can select people from Active Directory or an Outlook Address Book.

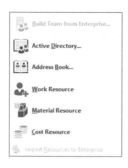

Properties

This group consists of three functions: Information, Notes and Details. Selecting Information will bring up the Resource Information dialog box, as illustrated below.

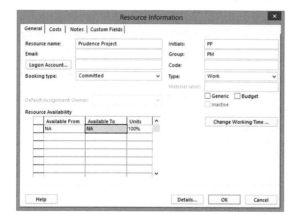

This allows information about the selected resource to be edited, the Change Working Time function (right-hand side above) allows changes to working days and hours and non-working time (such as vacations) to be input.

The Notes function allows text notes to be attached to a resource, while the Details function shows additional details for the selected resource.

Level

The final group contains six functions: Level Selection, Level Resource, Level All, Leveling Options, Clear Leveling and Next Overallocation. The leveling process is a technique to deal with overallocations (where a resource has too much work allocated to them) and is covered in Chapter 11.

Project

When the Project tab on the user interface is selected, the following project ribbon is displayed:

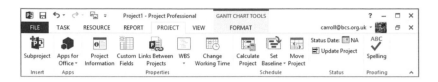

The ribbon is divided into seven groups, each of which contains one or more functions. Working from left to right, the groups are:

Insert

This group contains one function: Subproject. This feature allows you to insert another project file into the current project, as a subproject.

Apps

This group contains one function: Apps for Office. This feature displays a list of recently-used applications and See All which allows you to switch to or download applications for Office from the Office Store.

Properties

This group contains five functions: Project Information, Custom Fields, Links Between Projects, WBS (work breakdown structure) and Change Working Time.

Project Information is where you can set the start date and various other attributes for the project.

Custom Fields allows you to create your own fields and assign attributes (such as graphic indicators) to them.

Links Between Projects displays any external dependencies between the tasks in the current project and tasks in other projects.

WBS allows you to define or modify your own work breakdown structure and also renumber tasks.

Change Working Time allows you to set the overall working time and working/non-working days for the project, or for individual resources and tasks.

Schedule

This group contains three functions: Calculate Project, Set Baseline and Move Project. Calculate Project will re-schedule the project following any changes, if you have turned off calculation in the Project Options dialog box (see Chapter 11).

Set Baseline will bring up the Set Baseline dialog box (as illustrated right), which allows you to set a baseline or interim plan for the project or a range of selected tasks. It also has an option to clear a baseline or interim plan.

Move Project allows you to change the project start date and reschedule the project on this basis. It also has the option of moving any deadline dates.

Status

This group contains two functions: Status Date and Update Project. Status Date allows you to set the effective reporting date. This is the date (for example month end) that then appears on reports and is used for calculation purposes. If it is not changed, it defaults to the current date.

Update Project brings up the Update Project dialog box, which allows you to update progress on the entire project or on a selected range of tasks.

Proofing

The final group contains just one function: Spelling. This checks the spelling of all the text fields in the project.

View

When the View tab on the user interface is selected, the following view ribbon is displayed:

The ribbon is divided into seven groups, each of which contains one or more functions. Working across from left to right, these groups are:

Task Views

This group contains five functions: Gantt Chart, Task Usage, Network Diagram, Calendar and Other Views. Gantt Chart will bring up the default Gantt Chart view. Task Usage lists the tasks, with the resources assigned to them and the work scheduled. Network Diagram (an alternative to Gantt Chart view) has a box representing each task linked by dependency lines.

Calendar displays a monthly or weekly calendar, with the project tasks displayed on the dates where they are scheduled. Other Views lists the remaining, built-in, task views together with a More Views option (which brings up all 27 available views).

Resource Views

This group contains four functions: Team Planner, Resource Usage, Resource Sheet and Other Views. Team Planner (only available in Project Professional) provides a graphical schedule, which allows tasks to be dragged and dropped between resources, to assign or reassign them. Resource Usage lists resources with the tasks assigned to them and when they are scheduled. Resource Sheet lists all the resources with their full details. Other Views lists the remaining built-in resource views, together with a More Views option (which brings up all 27 available views).

Data

This group contains six functions: Sort, Outline, Tables, Highlight, Filter and Group. Sort brings up a list of sort options (start date, finish date, priority, cost or ID) and a Sort By option, which brings up the Sort dialog box. This enables a sort by multiple fields with ascending/descending options and the ability to renumber tasks or retain the existing outline structure.

Don't forget

Team Planner is only available in Project Professional.

Outline allows you to show or hide subtasks or select any outline level. Tables allows you to select from built in tables appropriate to the current view or More Tables, which allows you to select from the full list of 17 task tables and 10 resource tables. Highlight allows you to select from a range of built in highlight options (such as late tasks) or to select from a full range of all available options, including ranges. Group lets you group data by selecting from a range of built in options or from a full list of available options.

Zoom

This group contains four functions: Timescale, Zoom, Entire Project and Selected Tasks. Timescale allows you to select the granularity for the chart side of the view (e.g. days, weeks, months) or to use the Timescale dialog box to customize the timescale and the way in which non-working time is displayed (shaded).

Zoom allows you to zoom in or out of the current chart view. Entire Project brings the whole project into view. Selected Tasks is a useful feature that allows you to select one or more tasks on the table side and bring them into view on the chart side.

Split View

This group consists of two functions: Timeline and Details. If Timeline is selected, the timeline view is displayed above the Gantt chart. If Details is selected, the task form is displayed underneath the Gantt chart. Selecting either of these options will deselect the other option. Once either option is selected, a drop-down menu becomes available alongside it, so that any other available view can be selected to replace the default.

Window

This group consists of four functions: New Window, Switch Windows, Arrange All or Hide. New Window opens another view of the current project, and you can select from a drop down list of available views. Switch Windows lets you switch between open windows. Arrange All will tile all open windows side by side. Hide will hide the currently-selected window.

Macros

This group allows you to view and record macros, edit Visual Basic or define macro security.

Hot tip

Macro and Visual Basic are advanced functions that are outside the scope of this book.

Format

When the Format tab on the user interface is selected, the format ribbon that will be displayed will depend on the current view displayed. If the Gantt Chart view is currently displayed, the following format ribbon will be displayed:

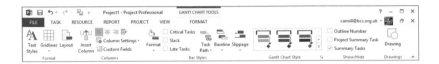

If the Task Usage view is selected, the following format ribbon will be displayed:

The following groups appear in these two format views, and many of the other format views as well:

Format

This group contains some or all Text Styles, Gridlines and Layout. Text Styles brings up the Text Styles dialog box, enabling the text style, size and color to be set. Gridlines enables the gridlines and progress lines on a chart to be defined. Layout enables the size and shape of bars and link lines to be defined.

Columns

This group contains Insert Column, Align Left/Center/Align Right, Wrap Text, Column Settings and Custom Fields. Insert Column displays a selection list for all the standard data fields that can be inserted, or the option to create a custom field. Align will format the text in the selected columns. Wrap Text will allow a long task name to be displayed by increasing the depth of the row. Column Settings allows columns to be hidden, text wrapped and formatted in detail. Custom Fields brings up the Custom Fields dialog box, allowing custom fields to be added and defined.

Bar Styles

This group contains Format, Critical Tasks, Slack, Late Tasks, Task Path, Baseline and Slippage. Format allows you to change the shape and color of a bar for a selected task, or the style for all tasks. Critical Tasks will turn all critical task bars red. Slack will insert a line to show any slack (float) time. Late Tasks will turn any late tasks bars black. Task Path will highlight predecessor or successor tasks of the selected task. Baseline will display a bar for the baseline (if set) under the task bar. Slippage will display a line in front of the task bar showing slippage from the baseline.

Gantt Chart Style

This group contains a selection of different colored styles and a link (bottom right) to the Bar Styles dialog box. Selecting any of the styles will change the color of the bars on the Gantt chart. The Bar Styles dialog box gives more detailed control over the appearance and color of bars.

Show/Hide

This group contains Outline Number, Project Summary Task and Summary Tasks. Outline Number will display a number in front of each task name in the format 1.1.1, representing the outline level of the task. Project Summary Task will insert a top-level task at the top of the sheet, with a summary bar on the chart. Selecting Summary Tasks will display all summary tasks (the default).

Drawings

This group contains only one function: Drawing, which enables you to insert or update a drawing on the chart. Selecting this produces a pop-up selection of drawing shapes and tools.

Details

This group contains Work, Actual Work, Cumulative Work, Baseline Work, Cost, Actual Cost and Add Details. Selecting any of the first six will add that information as another line under each task and resource. Add Details opens a detailed dialog box allowing you to select to show or hide any information and also format it.

Assignment

This group contains two functions: Information and Notes, which both bring up the Assignment Information dialog box (open at the General Information or Notes tabs). These allow you to amend the details of the assignment and to add notes.

The other views have similar format information, together with any view-specific formatting options.

Quick Access Toolbar

The Quick Access Toolbar is displayed in the top left-hand corner of the Project window, as illustrated below:

Project

In the illustration above, there are five icons. The first of these is the Project icon; selecting this will produce the drop-down menu (as illustrated on the right). These are the standard window functions and, strictly speaking, are not part of the Quick Access Toolbar.

Save

The next icon (representing a floppy disk) is the Save function. Selecting this saves the current version of the project.

Undo

The curly left arrow icon represents the Undo function. When it is active (not grayed out), selecting it will undo the last change made to the project.

Redo

The curly right arrow icon represents the Redo function. Selecting it will redo a change after it has been undone.

Customize Toolbar

The final icon is a drop-down arrow, which brings up the Customize Quick Access Toolbar (as illustrated on the right).

Any of the selected items (those with ticks beside them) can be deselected, and any of the other listed items can be selected to add them to the Quick Access Toolbar. More Commands will bring up a dialog box, as illustrated at the top of the page opposite. Show Below the Ribbon moves the Quick Access Toolbar to below the ribbon.

...cont'd

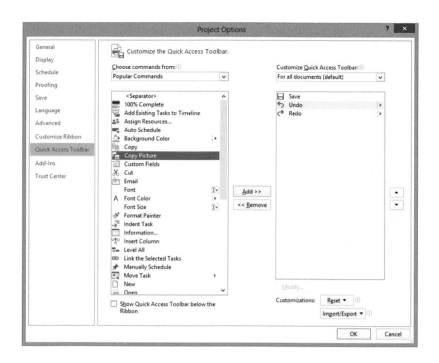

Changes can then be made to the Quick Access Toolbar, in the dialog box illustrated above, as follows:

1 Select any functions to be removed from the Quick Access Toolbar in the right-hand pane, and then click the Remove button in the middle

2 Select any functions from the popular commands in the left-hand pane to be added and click the Add button in the middle (Copy Picture has just been selected for addition in the illustration above)

3 To move any function up or down the list, select it in the right-hand pane and click the up or down arrows on the right-hand side

4 Click OK at the bottom to save the changes

Note that many more additional commands are available if the drop-down arrow beside popular commands, at the top, is selected.

Summary

- The Fluent User Interface (ribbon) contains seven tabs to bring up the File, Task, Resource, Report, Project, View and Format ribbons together with a Quick Access Toolbar

- File has the usual Save, Save As and Close functions as well as options for selecting recently-used files to open, creating a new file from a template, printing the current view, file information, sharing and exporting, together with account and program options

- Task has options for selecting the view, clipboard (cut, copy and paste), font changes, updating progress, scheduling options (manually or automatically scheduling tasks) and options for finding and editing content and formatting

- Resource has options for selecting the view, assigning resources to tasks, setting up a resource pool, adding and editing resources and leveling (the process of reallocating work to remove overloads)

- Project has options for inserting a subproject, accessing Office Apps (applications) setting the start date and other attributes for the project, defining custom fields, managing links between projects, defining a work breakdown structure, changing working time, scheduling, setting baselines, updating project status and spell checking

- View has options for selecting any of the 27 available views, sorting, grouping and filtering data, showing or hiding sub-tasks and summary tasks, showing a timeline or task details, arranging windows and macros

- Format has options for defining text styles, grid lines and layout, formatting columns and wrapping text, changing bar and chart styles, showing/hiding outline numbers, summary tasks and the project summary task, creating and editing drawings, selecting details to be displayed and editing assignment details

- Quick Access Toolbar is visible in all views, and it provides quick access to frequently-used commands. It can be customized, to add or remove commands

Managing your Project

This chapter introduces a structured approach to managing a project and explores some of the ways Project 2013 can help you manage your project.

A 4-Step Approach

Project management is the management of change.

In order to manage change, and, therefore, manage your project, you will need to perform a number of tasks. But, rather than just jumping straight in and starting to define these tasks, it is a good idea to take a more structured approach to a project.

These four steps will give you just that:

1 **Define the Objectives:** start by identifying what you are trying to achieve, the aims or goals of the project and where you want to get to by the end of the project

2 **Develop the Plan:** once you have defined the objectives, you can then plan how you are going to go about achieving them

3 **Carry it Out:** once you have planned the project, you will need to carry it out or manage it until the project is completed and the objectives have been achieved

4 **Hand it Over:** once you have completed the project, you have done your job as project manager and it is time to hand over the results of the project to whoever will be managing the process or system going forward

Unfortunately, a lot of projects seem to start at Step 3! It's what's known as the "Just Do It" school of management. But, even if you start your project at Step 2, what's the use of a plan if you don't know where you are going? So start at the beginning.

Interestingly, the difficult step for some project managers is the last one. They find it difficult to let go.

The project manager's job is to implement change. Once that change has been implemented, their role as project manager is completed. The new, changed state becomes a production process, and that requires production (rather than project) management.

In the remainder of this chapter, we will expand on each of these four steps and look at what is involved, starting with Step 1: Defining the Objectives.

Step 1: Define the Objectives

The first step in any project is to define the objectives. You need to do this in order to be able to:

- Make sure you have identified the right target

- Focus the other members of the project team on what the project is about

- Create team commitment to, and agreement about, the project objectives

- Ensure that you involve all interested parties in achieving a successful project outcome

SMART Objectives

When you set out to define your objectives, there is a useful acronym to remember: SMART. It stands for Strategic, Measurable, Agreed, Realistic and Timed.

Strategic

The objectives must address some strategic business purpose or need. If they do not, does the project really matter to the business and, if not, why carry it out?

Measurable

If you can't measure project achievement, how will you know if you've achieved anything? Reducing a process turn-round time from four to two hours is measurable as is reducing stock levels by 25% or even improving cash flow.

Agreed

If the rest of the business, and the rest of the project team, has not agreed with the objectives, there will be no commitment to achieving them. All key project stakeholders should agree them.

Realistic

There is no point in having objectives that are not achievable. If the objectives are not realistic, the project team will soon realize that and lose any commitment to the project.

Timed

Finally, the objectives must be timed. If there is no pressure to complete the project, it will never get completed. Improving the cash flow within six months is setting a time for achievement.

Hot tip

Some people use other words for SMART, such as Specific, Measurable, Assignable, Realistic and Time-Related. It doesn't matter, as long as they achieve a similar effect.

Hot tip

If you haven't already done so, define your project objectives now and make sure they are SMART.

Step 2: Develop the Plan

Having defined your project objectives, the next step is to plan how you will achieve them (how you will get there), by developing the project plan.

Before we start developing the plan, we need to look at some of the basic elements that make up a project plan. These are Tasks, Deliverables, Milestones and Resources:

Tasks

Tasks are the basic building blocks of the project. They represent the work that has to be carried out in order to complete the project. They will need to be carried out in some sort of timed sequence, and they will also be interdependent with one or more other tasks.

Deliverables

Deliverables (sometimes referred to as the products of a project) are the things that will be produced or delivered by the project along the way. Typically, they consist of progress or management reports, specifications of requirements, design documents and agreements, as well as the final result of the project (whatever that may be).

Milestones

Milestones are the points during the project where you can accurately measure the progress. They will typically be major events, such as an agreement of requirements, approval of funding or final acceptance.

Resources

Resources are the people and other things (material and finance) you will use on the project in order to carry out the tasks, produce the deliverables, and meet the milestones.

To put these into the context of the project plan, the plan will set out the *Tasks* needed to produce the *Deliverables* and complete the project. It will also set out the *Resources* you will need to carry out the tasks, and the *Milestones* you will use to measure your progress. The time line, or schedule, will set out when these things should happen.

The following topics in this chapter will look at Tasks, Deliverables, Milestones and Resources in more detail.

Hot tip

Deliverables provide the best way of measuring project progress.

Tasks and Deliverables

Any project consists of a number of tasks that need to be completed. Depending on the project, it may consist of very few tasks or it may involve very many tasks. Some of these tasks will be relatively short, while others will take much longer to complete. Some will be critical to the success of the project, while others may be less important.

Having defined or clarified the objectives, the first step in producing your project plan is to begin listing the key tasks; these are the important ones, the ones that are critical to the success of the project. They will typically be related to a key deliverable. For example, if you were building a house, there would be a "design" task, which would have the "house plans" as its deliverable.

The following example is for a feasibility study:

Key Tasks	Deliverables
Agree the Objectives	Objectives
Plan the Study	Study Plan
Information Gathering	Interview Notes
Produce Draft Requirements	Draft Requirements
Hold Feedback Sessions	Final Requirements
Develop Recommendations	Recommendations
Perform Risk Analysis	Risk Log
Produce Implementation Plan	Implementation Plan
Report to Management	Final Report

Milestones

Milestones are entered as dummy tasks, typically with a zero duration, as they mark a single point in time, as illustrated:

	Task Name	Duration	Start	S M T W T F S
7	Risk Analysis	1 day	08/19/13	
8	Implementation Plan	1 day	08/20/13	
9	Report to Management	1 day	08/21/13	
10	Study Completed	0 days	08/21/13	08/21

Hot tip

All the examples used in this book are available on our website. Go to **www.ineasysteps. com/resource-centre/ downloads/**

Step 3: Carry it Out

If you've been through Step 1 (Define the Objectives) and Step 2 (Develop the Plan), then you know where you're going (the Objectives) and you know how you are going to get there (the Plan). Now you can start carrying out the project by allocating the tasks to the people who will be doing them.

Resources

The key resources on most projects are the people who will be doing the work (including the project manager). In Project 2013, resources are entered in the Resource Sheet.

1 Click on the Resource tab and the down arrow beside Team Planner to open the list of built-in views, as illustrated on the right

2 Select Resource Sheet (fourth item on list) and the Resource Sheet view will open, as illustrated below:

Resource Name ▼	Type ▼	Material ▼	Initials ▼	Group ▼	Max. ▼	Std. Rate ▼
Prudence Project	Work		PP	PM	100%	$0.00/hr
Joe Soap	Work		JS	Marketing	100%	$0.00/hr
Mary Dee	Work		MD	Finance	100%	$0.00/hr
Wendy Page	Work		WP	IT	100%	$0.00/hr
Bill Buggs	Work		BB	Executive	100%	$0.00/hr

3 Type in the names, initials and groups for all the people who will be working on your project

4 If you have a human resource requirement, but don't yet know who it will be, just enter the role (e.g. Accountant) in the resource name column (you can change it later)

5 You can enter information in the other columns (not all illustrated above), if you have it, or leave the default values in for the time being

The resources defined above are all Work (this is the default for human resources or people). You can also define Material and Cost resources. These resource types are all covered in more detail in Chapter 7 (Resources).

Hot tip

All the examples used in this book are available on our website. Go to www.ineasysteps.com/resource-centre/downloads/

Hot tip

Get into the habit of saving your work before and after making any changes.

Step 4: Hand it Over

Once the project is completed, the project manager's role is finished. However, some project managers have problems with this final step.

Letting Go

You have to let go and let the people who will be responsible for the ongoing operation take over managing the process. They won't like it, or feel comfortable, if the project manager is looking over their shoulders the whole time, so let them get on with it. You should have planned any required training for them and, once they are up to speed, they will be fine.

Provide Support

But you cannot just drop a new process on the people who have to make it work and run! They will almost certainly have some problems adapting to new ways of doing things. What you must do is be available if they need you. This means scheduling some of your time to support the people carrying out the new process. This should only be for an initial, short, critical period (usually in the region of a month).

Finish the Paperwork

The handover time is a great opportunity to finish off any outstanding paperwork or documentation. Tidy up the project files and back everything up.

Project Review

The last scheduled task on the project should be to arrange and hold a post-implementation review. This is the time when you can go back to the original objectives and see if they have been achieved or not. Was there anything that happened during the project that could not be dealt with or included in the project? If there was, should another project be initiated to deal with it?

As part of this review, the methods and tools used on the project should also be examined, and anything learned should be noted for the benefit of future projects.

Thank the Team

Last, but not least, don't forget to thank everyone who helped you with the project – they will appreciate it. One of the nicest ways of thanking the project team is to take them out for a project team celebration meal.

Hot tip

Always invite your project sponsor and, with any luck, they will pick up the bill.

Summary

- Take a structured, 4-Step approach to project management: first define the objectives; second, develop the plan; then you can carry it out; and, finally, hand it over when it is completed

- When defining your objectives it is good to check if they are SMART: that means Strategic, Measurable, Agreed, Realistic and Timed

- Begin to develop your project plan by identifying the Tasks to be carried out, Deliverables that will be produced, the project Milestones that you will use to measure progress and the Resources you will need to do the work

- Try to identify all the critical, key (or important) tasks that need to be done, together with their associated deliverables, at the start of the project

- If you are not sure whether a task is a key task or not, include it anyway; it's safer than the risk of missing something which might be important

- In order to carry out the project, you will need to define the human (people) and other resources you will need on your project. Details of these are entered in Resource Sheet view. If you don't know who they will be yet, use a dummy name for the time being

- Get into the habit of saving your project file regularly when you are making changes to it

- Handing the project over can sometimes be difficult but it has to be done. It is a useful opportunity to tidy things up and make sure everything is in place for on-going support before handing it over

- Once everything has been handed over, it is then time to carry out a post-project review documenting how the project went compared to the original objectives and plan

- Finally, don't forget to thank the people who helped you on the project, including your project sponsor

4 Working with Tasks

Tasks represent the basic building blocks of a project, while milestones are the reference points used to measure progress. This chapter will illustrate the uses of tasks and milestones in creating the basic project plan.

Creating a Task

Tasks represent the basic building blocks of the project plan. They represent the pieces of work that will have to be done in order to carry out the project. Tasks can be entered in any view that includes a Task Name field, but the (default) Gantt Chart view is the easiest one to use in the build up of the task list.

1 Open a project file, or to create a new one, select the Task tab and Gantt Chart view (if you are not already in it)

Auto Schedule

You can insert tasks either using auto scheduling or manual scheduling. For auto scheduling:

2 Click on Mode (as illustrated above) and select Auto Schedule

3 Click in the first Task Name field, type in the task name (e.g. Agree Project Objectives) and then press Enter

A Task ID (identity) of 1 is assigned to the task (on the left-hand side above) and the default duration of 1 day is allocated. The question mark after the duration indicates that it is the default (estimated) duration. The task is scheduled to start on today's date (or the start date of the project, if you have changed it) and a 1 day bar is shown on the Gantt chart to the right. Non-working days on the Gantt chart are shaded.

Hot tip

The collapsed view on the right was produced by reducing the depth of the window.

Manual Schedule

If manual scheduling mode is selected in place of auto scheduling (at Step 2 opposite) and the task name is entered (as in Step 3 opposite), the following is the result:

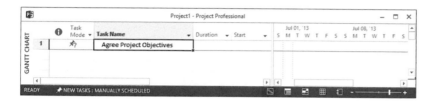

As can be seen, the task ID of 1 is allocated and the task name is inserted, but no duration or start date is assumed. In manual schedule mode you would need to enter these manually. This mode is useful if you have identified the tasks but have not yet estimated the durations, or when they will be scheduled.

Wrap Text

If the task name you type in is longer than the width of the column, the text will wrap to the next line, as in the following illustration:

Hot tip

Keep task names short but meaningful.

If you do not want the text to wrap, you can make the column wider by dragging the edge of the column header to the right, as illustrated.

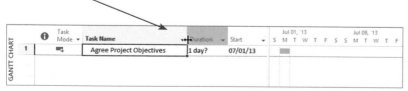

Wrap text is the default setting, but it can be changed by de-selecting the Wrap Text function (as illustrated right) on the Format tab. Any extra text will be hidden from view unless the Task Name column width is adjusted.

Hot tip

You can also select and de-select wrap text by right clicking on the task name header.

45

Task Duration

When Auto Schedule is selected, new tasks are created with an estimated duration of one day. The estimated duration is indicated by the question mark after "1 day" in the Duration field. Once you enter a duration, the question mark will be removed. The duration can be changed by using the spin controls or by typing directly into the field.

1 Click on the Duration field and use the spin controls (the up and down arrows that appear when the field is selected) to increase or reduce it

Note, in the illustration above, that the bar on the Gantt chart is showing the duration as six working days (Saturday and Sunday being non-working days by default).

You can also click on the Duration field and type in a number. It will default to the existing time type (days in this example).

2 To change the duration time type, you need to enter the number followed by m (minutes), h (hours), d (days), w (weeks) or mo (months)

Note, in the illustration above, that 24 hours is scheduled to take three working days. The default is eight hours working time per day, so 24 hours is three working days.

3 If you need to enter an elapsed time (rather than working time) duration, you can do so by typing an "e" in front of the time type, so "24eh" will be interpreted and scheduled as illustrated below:

Adding Tasks

Additional tasks can be added to a project at any time. The tasks can be added after existing tasks, or inserted in between or in front of existing tasks. We will look at doing both.

1 To add new tasks to the end, click on the first blank Task Name field and type in your new task name, press the tab key, type in the duration and then press Enter

2 To insert a new task into an existing task list, click on the task name that you wish to insert the new task in front of, then click New Task on the Task ribbon

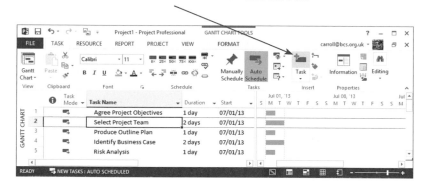

3 Type in the new task name, tab to the duration field and enter the duration

The new task is inserted in the selected position, as illustrated above. Continue to add tasks as above while you build up your task list.

47

Hot tip

You can also use the keyboard Insert key as a short-cut for inserting a new task.

Task Dependencies

Tasks do not exist in isolation, most will be dependant on one or more other tasks, and they will have one or more other tasks dependant on them. The only exceptions are the first and last task in the project.

In the following illustration, Task 2 requires something from and is therefore dependant on Task 1 being completed before it can begin. In a similar way, Task 3 is dependant on Task 2.

In Project, you create these dependencies by linking the appropriate tasks. Linking tasks allows you to specify the circumstances where the start or finish of a task is dependant on the start or finish of another task or set of tasks.

Finish-to-start

The most common type of dependency or link is the finish-to-start dependency (as illustrated above), where the finish of Task 1 allows Task 2 to start. Typically, this is where Task 2 needs something that is produced in Task 1.

On the Gantt chart, the link is shown as illustrated on the right.

There are three other types of links:

Start-to-start

This is where Task 2 can start at the same time as Task 1 and can take place at the same time. It is shown on the Gantt chart as illustrated right.

Finish-to-finish

This is used where Task 2 has to finish at the same time as Task 1 and is shown as illustrated right.

Start-to-finish

In this case, when Task 1 starts Task 2 must finish and is shown as illustrated on the right.

These three (and particularly the last one) are likely to be the exception rather than the rule.

Beware

It is best to avoid the start-to-finish link, if possible, as it can cause some problems.

Linking Tasks

Task dependencies are created by linking tasks. The default dependency is the finish-to-start dependency, and this will normally be the way you will want to link most of the tasks in your project. The quickest approach is to link all the tasks in this way to start with and then make any required changes.

1 In Gantt Chart view, click on the Task Name column header to select all your tasks

	ⓘ	Task Name	Duration	Start	Jul 01, '13 S M T W T F S	Jul 08, '13 S M T W T F S
1		Agree Project Objectives	1 day	07/01/13	▬	
2		Identify Stakeholders	1 day	07/01/13	▬	
3		Select Project Team	2 days	07/01/13	▬	
4		Produce Outline Plan	1 day	07/01/13	▬	
5		Identify Business Case	2 days	07/01/13	▬	
6		Risk Analysis	1 day	07/01/13	▬	

2 Click the Link Tasks function (as illustrated on the right) on the Task ribbon

3 Click the Respect Links function (as illustrated on the right) on the Task ribbon

	ⓘ	Task Name	Duration	Start	Jul 01, '13 S M T W T F S	Jul 08, '13 S M T W T F S	Jul 15, '13 S M T W T F S
1		Agree Project Objectives	1 day	07/01/13			
2		Identify Stakeholders	1 day	07/02/13			
3		Select Project Team	2 days	07/03/13			
4		Produce Outline Plan	1 day	07/05/13			
5		Identify Business Case	2 days	07/08/13			
6		Risk Analysis	1 day	07/10/13			

The tasks are now all linked in a finish-to-start dependency. The start dates are adjusted so that each task starts when its predecessor finishes.

You can also link tasks by holding down the Ctrl key, clicking the individual task names, and then clicking the Link Tasks button.

Links are always created in the direction in which you select the tasks. Selecting Task 2 and then Task 1 will result in a link from Task 2 to Task 1. Task 1 will then be dependent on Task 2.

4 If you are happy with the way your tasks are linked, save your project file before you start changing anything else

Unlinking Tasks

If you have just completed the previous topic, you will have linked all the tasks in the project in a finish-to-start dependency. You may now need to unlink some of them.

1 Select the two tasks you wish to unlink (hold down the Ctrl key and click on the two task names)

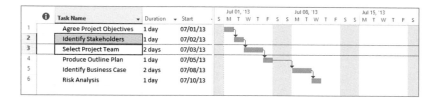

2 Click the Unlink Tasks function (as illustrated right) on the Task ribbon and the link is removed, as illustrated below

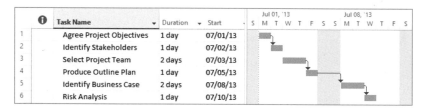

3 An alternative way of accessing the link between tasks is to double-click on the link between the two tasks you wish to unlink on the Gantt chart. This will open the Task Dependency dialog box

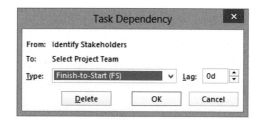

4 Click Delete and the link is removed

You can also unlink several tasks at the same time by selecting them all and then clicking the Unlink button.

Changing Dependencies

Although the majority of tasks in a project will normally be in a finish-to-start dependency, you will sometimes need to change the dependency to one of the other types.

1 In Gantt Chart view, double-click on the link between the two tasks where you wish to change the dependency. This will bring up the Task Dependency dialog box

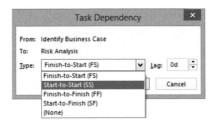

2 Click on the down arrow to the right of Type to bring up the drop-down list of options (as illustrated above)

3 Select the required option and click OK

In the following illustration, Start-to-Start (SS) was selected at Step 3 above and the two tasks have now been rescheduled to start on the same day:

		Task Name	Duration	Start																				
					Jul 01, '13							Jul 08, '13							Jul 15, '13					
					S	M	T	W	T	F	S	S	M	T	W	T	F	S	S	M	T	W	T	F	S
1		Agree Project Objectives	1 day	07/01/13																				
2		Identify Stakeholders	1 day	07/02/13																				
3		Select Project Team	2 days	07/03/13																				
4		Produce Outline Plan	1 day	07/05/13																				
5		Identify Business Case	2 days	07/08/13																				
6		Risk Analysis	1 day	07/08/13																				

The four types of dependency were defined on page 48 (Task Dependencies). Selecting Finish-to-Finish (FF) or Start-to-Finish (SF) will link the tasks as illustrated on that page.

To change the dependency back to the way it was originally, repeat steps one and two above and select Finish-to-Start (FS) from the drop-down list.

Selecting (None) on the drop-down list of options removes the dependency and is, therefore, another way of unlinking tasks.

Don't forget

All the examples used in this book are available on our website. Go to **www.ineasysteps. com/resource-centre/ downloads/**

Moving a Task

If you wish to move a task to a new position in the task list, the easiest way is to use drag-and-drop. Select the ID of the task that you want to move and drag it to its new position.

1 Click once on the Task ID of the task you want to move, to select the whole task, and then release the mouse button

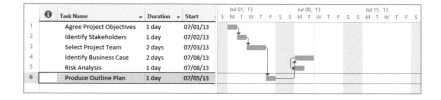

2 Now, click on the task ID again, but this time do not release the mouse button and drag the task up or down the task list as required. Notice the insertion point marker (see shaded line next to the pointer above) as you drag

3 When you get to the desired new location, release the mouse button

The task is moved to its new location (as illustrated above) and the links have been retained. You may wish to change them if they are no longer appropriate.

4 To re-link the task in its new position, you could remove the existing links and replace them with links from Tasks 4 and 5 to Task 6, which will reschedule the moved task (as illustrated below)

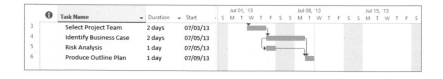

Deleting a Task

If you need to delete a task from a task list, simply select it and delete it as follows:

1 Select the task to be deleted by clicking on its Task ID, which selects the whole task

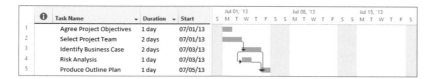

2 Then press the keyboard Delete key and the task is removed from the project

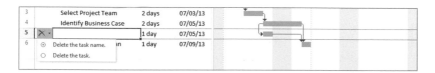

3 If you delete the wrong task (or tasks) in error, you can reverse your previous actions using the Undo function (as illustrated right) on the Quick Access Toolbar

4 You can also delete individual fields or whole tasks by selecting the Task Name and pressing the Delete key. This will bring up a smart tag asking you to confirm what you want to delete (see below)

5 Click on "Delete the task name" to just clear that field, or "Delete the task" and the whole task will be deleted

As with Step 3, if you make a mistake you can always use the Undo function on the Quick Access Toolbar.

Task Form

Task Form view (which displays the task details) is one of the built-in views available in Project. It is used to enter, view and edit details of individual tasks.

1 Click on the arrow next to Gantt Chart view on the Task ribbon to display the built-in views (as illustrated on the right) and select Task Form to display this view

Although this view is useful to work on task details, there is another option:

2 Click the View tab to display the View ribbon (as illustrated below)

3 Select the Details option in the Split View group and the Task Form is displayed in the lower half of the screen (as illustrated below)

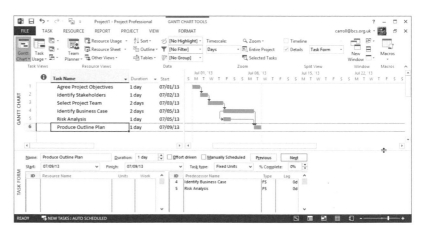

4 You can now view, enter and edit task details directly in the lower pane, and any changes made in either pane will be reflected in the other

5 The split bar (shown in gray, with a move cursor on the right-hand side in the illustration above) can be moved up or down as required and double-clicking on it will hide the Task Form and return to the basic Gantt Chart view

Project Milestones

Milestones represent significant events that mark the progress of a project. Any task can be made a milestone by setting the duration to zero or you can insert a milestone on the Task ribbon:

1 Select the task you want to insert a milestone in front of, and then click the Insert Milestone function on the Task ribbon

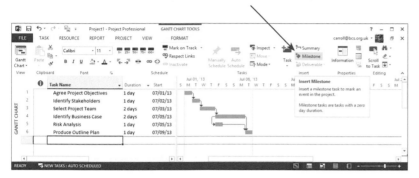

2 Type in the milestone name and link any tasks the milestone is dependant on

	❶	Task Name	Duration	Start
1		Agree Project Objectives	1 day	07/01/13
2		Identify Stakeholders	1 day	07/02/13
3		Select Project Team	2 days	07/03/13
4		Identify Business Case	2 days	07/05/13
5		Risk Analysis	1 day	07/05/13
6		Produce Outline Plan	1 day	07/09/13
7		Project Approval	0 days	07/09/13

3 To add a duration to the milestone, click in the Duration field and enter a duration, then click the Information function (to the right of Insert Milestone) on the Task ribbon to open the Task Information dialog box

4 Select the Advanced tab, check "Mark task as milestone" (bottom left) and click OK. The task will be shown as a milestone with a duration (as illustrated below)

	❶	Task Name	Duration	Start
1		Agree Project Objectives	1 day	07/01/13
2		Identify Stakeholders	1 day	07/02/13
3		Select Project Team	2 days	07/03/13
4		Identify Business Case	2 days	07/05/13
5		Risk Analysis	1 day	07/05/13
6		Produce Outline Plan	1 day	07/09/13
7		Project Approval	5 days	07/10/13

You can also double-click the Task Name to open the Task Information dialog box.

Recurring Tasks

Any task that is regularly repeated in a project is called a recurring task. It could be a project team meeting, a meeting with your project sponsor or the production of a monthly report.

The procedure for setting up a recurring task is different from creating a normal task, and you cannot convert a normal task into a recurring task.

1 To insert a recurring task, click the down arrow beneath the Insert Task function on the Task ribbon, select Recurring Task and the Recurring Task Information dialog box will open (as illustrated below)

2 Enter the Task Name, Duration, Recurrence and Range information (as in the above example) and click OK

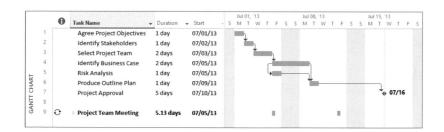

The recurring task is inserted into the task list. The triangle next to the task name indicates that it consists of a number of subtasks (one for each meeting in this case). Clicking on the triangle will display the individual meeting sub-tasks. Double-clicking on the task name will bring up the Recurring Task Information dialog box again, to allow any further editing.

Beware

The duration of this summary task is the working days from the start of the first meeting to the end of the final one.

56

Inactive Tasks

Tasks created in Project are, by default, active tasks. That is to say their work effort, resources and costs are recorded in the project. From time to time there may be tasks that may only be required if certain events occur.

As an example: if a project risk occurs it may be necessary to carry out a number of tasks to rectify the results of the risk and these may have been identified as a result of risk analysis and contingency planning. Once identified, they can now be input to Project as inactive tasks and activated later if the risk occurs.

1 Create any new task or tasks at an appropriate place in the project as illustrated below

2 Select the task(s) and click on the Inactivate button on the Task ribbon (as illustrated right) and the inactivated tasks are now rendered in gray with a line through the task data, as illustrated below

	🛈	Task Name	Duration	Start	Jul 15, '13 S M T W T F S	Jul 22, '13 S M T W T F S
6		Produce Outline Plan	1 day	07/09/13		
7		Project Approval	5 days	07/10/13	◆ 07/16	
8		Revise Outline Plan	2 days	07/17/13		
9		Resubmit	1 day	07/19/13		
10		Plan Next Stage	2 days	07/17/13		

The inactive tasks do not impact on the scheduling of subsequent tasks. If the tasks are no longer required at any time they can be deleted without any impact on the project. However, if they are required they can be reactivated as follows:

3 Select the task(s) to be reactivated and click the Inactivate button on the Task ribbon. The tasks are reactivated and re-included in the schedule, resulting in the rescheduling of any subsequent tasks, as illustrated below

	🛈	Task Name	Duration	Start	Jul 15, '13 S M T W T F S	Jul 22, '13 S M T W T F S
6		Produce Outline Plan	1 day	07/09/13		
7		Project Approval	5 days	07/10/13	◆ 07/16	
8		Revise Outline Plan	2 days	07/17/13		
9		Resubmit	1 day	07/19/13		
10		Plan Next Stage	2 days	07/22/13		

Summary

- Tasks are the basic building blocks of a project plan and they are best entered in Gantt Chart view

- Auto schedule allows Project to schedule the start date of a task, while manual schedule allows you to enter the start date

- If the task name is too large for the column, Project will wrap the text to the next line unless you override it

- Task duration can be defined in minutes, hours, days, weeks or even months and it can be typed in or set using the spinner controls

- Tasks can be added to the end of a task list or they can be inserted using the New Task function (or the Insert key); they will be inserted in front of the selected task

- There are four types of task dependency: finish-to-start is the most common dependency, but tasks can also be linked in finish-to-finish, start-to-start or start-to-finish

- Tasks are linked to form dependencies using Link Task and can also be unlinked using Unlink Task

- Task dependencies can be changed or deleted by double-clicking on the link between the tasks

- Tasks can be moved up or down the task list by selecting the task and dragging it up or down to its new place. You may also need to change the dependency links after this move

- Tasks can be deleted using the Delete key and smart tag

- The undo button can reverse any mistakes you may make

- The task form can be applied to the Gantt chart to give more detail and control over a task

- Project milestones are created as tasks with zero duration or they can be set through the Task Information dialog box

- Recurring tasks need to be set up using Insert Recurring Task from the Task ribbon

- Tasks that may not be required can be inactivated so they don't impact the schedule unless they are required

5 Adding Structure

In this chapter, we start to add some structure to the project by developing summary tasks and subtasks and using outlining.

Project Structure

A simple project, such as carrying out a feasibility study, might consist of no more than 10 or 12 tasks. A medium-sized project, such as introducing a new business venture or planning and organizing an exhibition, could run into over one hundred individual tasks. While a very large project, such as building a new airport, could run into many thousands of tasks.

Work Breakdown Structure

If you try to identify and plan every single task in your project right from the start, you will almost certainly be doomed to failure. In the early stages of a project there are just too many uncertainties and unknown factors, which will only become known as the project progresses. To cope with this, a project needs to be broken down into manageable chunks, one level at a time. This is known as the Work Breakdown Structure (WBS).

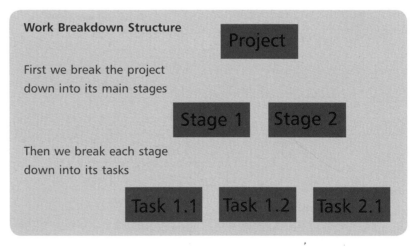

Work Breakdown Structure

Project

First we break the project down into its main stages

Stage 1   Stage 2

Then we break each stage down into its tasks

Task 1.1   Task 1.2   Task 2.1

1 First break your project down into discrete chunks, with their own major deliverables, these are usually referred to as Stages (but they may also be called Phases)

2 Then, in turn, break each Stage into the Tasks that will be needed to carry it out

3 Finally, each Task may also need to be broken down into one (or more) level of Subtasks (not shown in the diagram above), depending on the size of the project and the size of the task

Summary Tasks

In Microsoft Project, structure is implemented through Subtasks and Summary Tasks. Any task that has a subtask is itself a summary task. Therefore, a task can be a subtask of another task and a summary task itself. Project Stages are summary tasks.

A summary task is created in similar way to any other task but its subtasks are indented.

1 Select the tasks you want to insert a summary task for and then click on Insert Summary Task on the Task ribbon

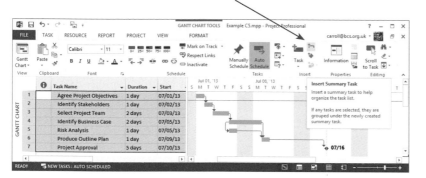

The new summary task is inserted and the selected tasks have been made its subtasks, as illustrated below:

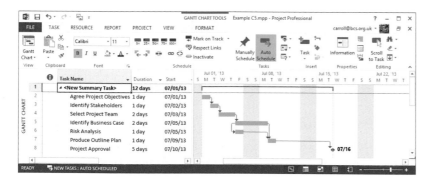

2 Type in the name for the summary task and press Enter, the job is done

Note that individual tasks can also be promoted to summary tasks or demoted to sub-tasks by selecting the task and using the Indent Task and Outdent Task functions on the Task ribbon (as illustrated on the right)

Project Stages

Conventionally, in project management methodology, the first-level summary tasks are referred to as project stages.

Project management methodology initially grew out of the construction industry, and it still retains some of that industry's terminology. In later years, it has also been influenced by the information technology industry, which, interestingly, has a lot of similarities.

Using that influence, we can now build a little further on our 4-step approach by expanding our second step (plan how we will get there) into two separate stages. The first is to determine what the detailed business needs are and the second is to define what we will need to do to achieve those needs.

If this sounds a bit like "overkill", keep an open mind for the time being. Hopefully, as we develop the process further, you will begin to see why this is a useful approach. These five project stages are conventionally referred to as:

Initiation
To define the project objectives and the team structure, produce the initial (outline) project plan and get the project started.

Strategy
To determine what the detailed business needs are and what the potential payback will be when we achieve them.

Analysis
To define what will need to be done in order to meet the business needs.

Design and Build
Carrying out the project by doing the detailed design of how it will be done and then doing it (i.e. build it, buy it, etc.).

Implementation
To install and hand over the new process and close the project.

The chief benefit of this approach is that the major expense or effort usually occurs in the Design and Build stage. At each of the preceding stages, the potential investment and benefits can be reappraised to ensure that it will still be viable. If not, the project can be wound up with minimal cost to the business.

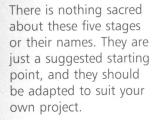

Hot tip

There is nothing sacred about these five stages or their names. They are just a suggested starting point, and they should be adapted to suit your own project.

...cont'd

Adding Project Stages

Having decided on the number of stages, you can initially add them to the project with a dummy task under each. These can be replaced later, when you have identified the real tasks.

1   If you have not already created the first project stage in the Summary Task topic (page 61), do it now

2   Then select the Task where you want to insert your next stage and click the Insert Summary Task function in the Task ribbon

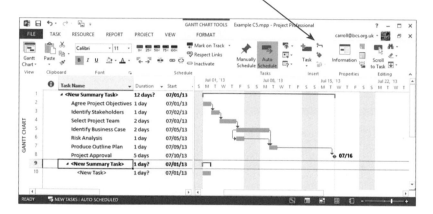

In the example above, there were no existing tasks where the new stage was inserted so Project has inserted a dummy task as well. Note that the new stage has been inserted at the same level as the preceding task, so it will need to be outdented.

3   Type in the stage name, dummy task name, dummy task duration and outdent the stage, if required, using Outdent Task, as illustrated right

4   Link the last task in the first stage to the first task in the second stage

Continue inserting stages (and dummy tasks, with durations where required) and linking them as above. Ideally, all the tasks in the project should be linked and, on completion, your project should look something like the first illustration on the following page (overleaf).

Changing the Timescale

Once you begin to link all the tasks in a project, they will quickly vanish off the timescale in the right-hand pane and you won't be able to see the whole project. This is easily remedied.

1 Select the View tab and click on Entire Project on the View ribbon to bring the whole project into view

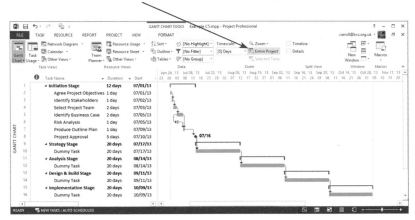

2 Click on the Task Name header to select all tasks, click Outline on the View ribbon and select Level 1 from the drop-down list (as illustrated right), to display the top-level view of your project, with just the stages showing (as illustrated below)

You can use Outline > All Subtasks from the View ribbon to bring all the tasks back into view, and use Zoom > Zoom In, Zoom Out and Custom from the View ribbon to get more or less details into view. Finally, select Timescale > Days from the View ribbon to get back to a days within weeks view (as illustrated below):

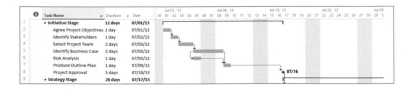

Outline Numbering

For a small project with very few tasks, the Task ID number is probably a good enough way of numbering your tasks. But, for larger projects, a more structured way of numbering, that reflects the Work Breakdown Structure (WBS), will be needed. Outline numbering gives you a simple way of achieving this.

1 Select the Format tab and click Outline Numbering on the Format ribbon

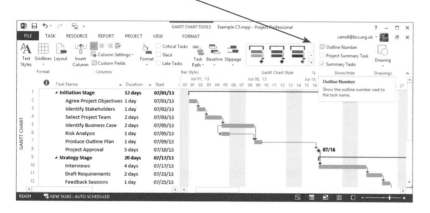

Your stages and tasks will now be numbered in a structured format. Stages being numbered 1, 2, 3, etc. and tasks being numbered 1.1, 1.2, 1.3, etc. (as illustrated below).

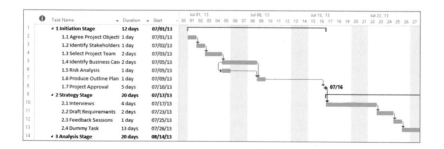

If an additional level of subtasks is inserted below task 1.3, they will be numbered 1.3.1, 1.3.2 and so on.

One result of the addition of the numbers to the task name is that some of the task names may get truncated. You could resolve this by selecting Wrap Text from the Format ribbon, or by increasing the size of the field by dragging the edge of the Task Name header (as illustrated on page 45).

Subtasks

Creating additional layers of subtasks is a similar process to creating summary tasks, but, instead of inserting a summary task and outdenting it, we insert the subtasks and indent them. This then turns the task above them into a summary task.

1 Select the task in front of which you wish to insert the subtasks and then click Insert Task on the Task ribbon once for each new subtask to be inserted:

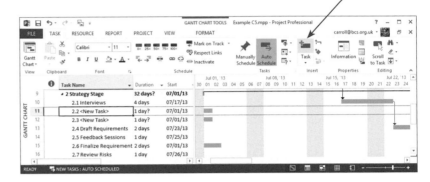

2 Type in the new subtask names and their durations (in the example below, Interview Managers and Interview Staff, both with 2 days duration)

Notice that they have been treated as tasks at the same level as the task above them and that they have not been linked or indented:

3 Select the two tasks by Ctrl + clicking on them and clicking Indent Task on the Task ribbon

The two subtasks have now been numbered 2.1.1 and 2.1.2 and their summary task 2.1 is now in bold (as illustrated below).

As can be seen from the above illustration, the tasks have not yet been linked, so we need to complete that step:

4 Select the two tasks and click the Link function on the Task ribbon to link the two tasks

As can be seen from the illustration above, the subtasks are now linked but the summary task (2.1 Interviews) has the links from and to the preceding and succeeding tasks. Ideally, these links should be changed to go to and from the new subtasks to maintain task dependencies at the lowest level:

5 Delete the links to the summary task and add new links from and to the preceding and succeeding tasks:

Hot tip

When building up a stage schedule, it is a good idea to include some contingency for the (as yet) unknown.

67

Summary

- The way the tasks in a project are structured is referred to as the Work Breakdown Structure (WBS). The best approach is to break the project down one stage and one level at a time, as more information becomes known

- A summary task is any task that has subtasks beneath it, and, with multiple levels, a task can be both a subtask and a summary task

- Outdenting is the process in Project that promotes a task to a summary task, while indenting is the process that demotes a task to a subtask

- The first-level tasks in a structure are normally called the project stages and are always summary tasks. There will normally be between three and eight stages in a project and a standard set of five (Initiation, Strategy, Analysis, Design & Build, and Implementation) are suggested as a starting point

- Stages are created in a project by inserting them as summary tasks and indenting the tasks beneath them to make them subtasks of the stage

- As you start to build up your project structure, you can zoom in and out to change the timescale and show different outline levels. This facility lets you move between the big picture and the detail

- Although you can create a custom WBS in Project, the built in outline numbering function can provide a simple, numeric reference, which reflects the WBS at each level

- Subtasks are created by inserting new tasks below an existing task and then indenting them

- As you start to build up your project plan, it is a good idea to include some contingency at the end of each stage to reflect the unknown things that will only be discovered later in the project

- Task dependencies (the links between tasks) should always be created between the bottom level tasks rather than at the summary task level

6 More About Tasks

This chapter goes into Tasks in a little more detail. It introduces lag time and lead time, task notes, setting deadline dates, critical path and moving linked tasks.

Lag Time and Lead Time

Up to now we have been linking tasks, mainly in a finish-to-start dependency, with the next task starting immediately after the preceding task finishes. However, there are times when you will want the tasks to have a gap or overlap between them, and we do this by using lag time and lead time.

Lag Time

Lag time is when there is a gap (or lag) between the finish of one task and the start of the next task. This is input using the Lag field on the Task Dependency dialog box. In the following example, we want to introduce a 2 day lag between the end of Task 1.1 Agree Project Objectives and the start of Task 1.2 Identify Stakeholders.

1 Double-click on the line connecting the two tasks where you want to add lag time to open the Task Dependency dialog box

2 Change the Lag time using the spinner controls, or by typing in the required duration, and click OK

The dependent task will be rescheduled and the link line will be extended to the length of the lag time. Any other tasks linked to the dependant task will also be rescheduled by Project.

Lead Time

Lead time is where there is an overlap, with the next task starting before the previous task has finished. This is also input using the Lag field, but using a negative number to represent lead time. In the following example, we want to introduce a 1 day lead time between Task 1.3 Select Project Team and Task 1.4 Identify Business Case.

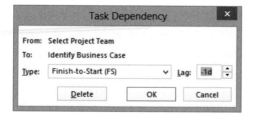

	❶	Task Name	▼	Duration	▼	Start	
1		◢ 1 Initiation Stage		14 days		07/01/13	
2		1.1 Agree Project Objectives		1 day		07/01/13	
3		1.2 Identify Stakeholders		1 day		07/04/13	
4		1.3 Select Project Team		2 days		07/05/13	
5		1.4 Identify Business Case		2 days		07/09/13	
6		1.5 Risk Analysis		1 day		07/09/13	
7		1.6 Produce Outline Plan		1 day		07/11/13	

1 Double-click on the connecting line between the two tasks where you want to include lead time to open the Task Dependency dialog box

Task Dependency ✕

From: Select Project Team
To: Identify Business Case
Type: Finish-to-Start (FS)   Lag: -1d

Delete   OK   Cancel

2 Change the Lag time using the down spinner control, or type a negative number to represent the lead time duration, and click OK

	❶	Task Name	▼	Duration	▼	Start	
1		◢ 1 Initiation Stage		13 days		07/01/13	
2		1.1 Agree Project Objectives		1 day		07/01/13	
3		1.2 Identify Stakeholders		1 day		07/04/13	
4		1.3 Select Project Team		2 days		07/05/13	
5		1.4 Identify Business Case		2 days		07/08/13	
6		1.5 Risk Analysis		1 day		07/08/13	
7		1.6 Produce Outline Plan		1 day		07/10/13	

The dependent task has been brought forward and now starts one day before the preceding task finishes. In the above example, the task following the dependant task has also been brought forward to overlap by one day, due to its start-to-start dependency.

Task Inspector

Task Inspector allows you to view constraints and dependencies that impact a task's start date. They can help to establish the factor or factors that may be delaying a task, such as task dependency, calendar constraints, schedule date, holidays or vacation.

1 In Gantt Chart view, click Inspect on the Task's ribbon to open the Task Inspector panel to the left of the task sheet

In the example above, the Task Inspector panel displays the name, start and finish dates of the selected task. It also contains details of the predecessor task(s), the dependency type, any lag time and the calendar(s) that are applied. The predecessor task(s) and calendar(s) are active hypertext links (shown in blue).

2 Click on the predecessor task name to back-track to that task

3 Click on the calendar name to display the relevant resource or project calendar

4 Click on the arrow alongside Inspect on the Task ribbon and the drop down menu illustrated below right gives some additional options

The three additional options will, if selected, result in indicators being flagged on all tasks where: there is a potential problem requiring action; there is a suggested improvement that could be made; or a problem warning has been ignored.

Task Notes

Task notes can be attached to any task, to record additional, free text information. You can add a note to a task in Gantt Chart view, or any other view where the Note function is active on the Task ribbon.

1 Select the task that you wish to add the note to

2 Click the Notes function on the Task ribbon to open the Task Information dialog box at the Notes tab, as illustrated below

3 Type in your note and format it, if required, (using the format buttons above the typing area), then click OK to add the note to the task

4 Now pause your mouse pointer over the yellow note symbol in the task's information box to display the note

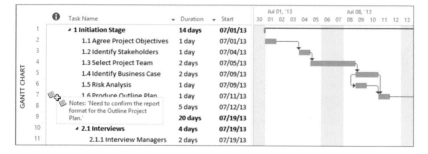

5 To edit the note or add further text to it, just double-click the yellow note symbol in the information box. This will reopen the Task Information dialog box at the note

6 To delete a note, just delete all the note text in the Task Information dialog box

You can also access task notes text by double-clicking on the task name (or clicking Information on the Task ribbon and selecting the Notes tab).

Deadline Dates

Deadline dates can be set on a task to indicate a date by which the task must be completed. If, at any time, the task slips, so that it will not be completed by its deadline date, a warning indicator will be displayed in the information box for the task.

Deadline dates are for information only and do not have any impact on the scheduling process. They should not be confused with task constraints (dealt with in Chapter 11), which can determine when a task will be scheduled. Deadline dates are set on the Advanced tab of the Task Information dialog box.

1 In Gantt Chart view, double-click on the task you want to set a deadline for and the Task Information dialog box will open

2 Select the Advanced tab (as illustrated above), click on the down arrow beside Deadline, select your deadline date and click OK. The deadline is indicated by a green arrow symbol on the Gantt chart:

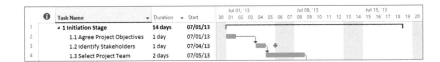

If the task slips past its deadline date, a warning indicator will be displayed in the task's information box. If you position your cursor over the warning indicator, the details will be displayed:

Moving Around

As your project starts to build up, you will soon reach a point where you will not be able to see all the project information in one view, particularly in Gantt Chart view. As well as zooming in and out (which was covered in Chapter 5), you will also need to be able to move around the view.

Scrollbars

You can use the scroll bars and sliders to move around vertically and horizontally. Gantt Chart view has one vertical scrollbar (on the right-hand side of the screen), which moves the task sheet and the Gantt chart information up and down. It has two horizontal scroll bars (at the bottom of the screen), which move the task sheet and the chart left and right independently of each other.

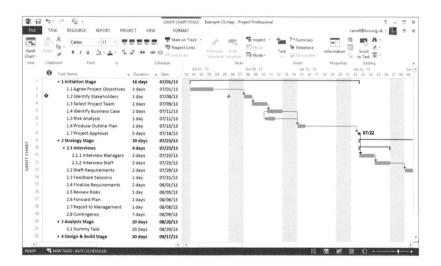

Scroll To Task

When moving around with the scroll bars, it is quite easy to lose all sight of the Gantt chart part of the view. A useful short-cut is Scroll To Task, which will bring the appropriate part of the Gantt chart into view.

1 Click on the task(s) you want to bring into view in the task sheet and click Scroll To Task on the Task ribbon

The Gantt chart will scroll to bring the bar(s) for the selected task(s) into view on the right-hand side of the screen.

Hot tip

You can use Ctrl + Home at any time to get back to the top left-hand corner of any view.

Critical Path

The critical path is the term given to the sequence of tasks that are critical to the duration of the project. The following diagram represents a simple project consisting of four tasks.

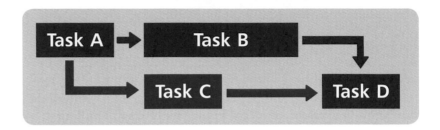

Tasks A, C and D are each of one days' duration, while Task B is of two day's duration. Tasks B and C are both dependent on Task A, with finish-to-start relationships. Task D is dependent on both Tasks B and C, again with finish-to-start relationships. Assuming no lag time, the total duration of the project is four days.

Critical Tasks
If Task C was to slip by one day, it would still not impact the completion of Task D and, therefore, the project would still be completed in four days. Task C is, therefore, a non-critical task. On the other hand, if any of Tasks A, B or D were to slip by one day, the project would take five days to complete and these tasks are, therefore, critical tasks.

Calculating the Critical Path
The critical path is the path through the project that links all of the critical tasks. Calculating the critical path in Project is done through the Critical Tasks function on the Format ribbon.

 With your project in Gantt Chart view, select the Format tab and click Critical Tasks

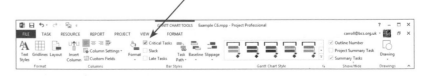

The default when setting the critical path is that critical tasks will be displayed in red and non-critical tasks in blue. The results of setting the critical path is illustrated top right.

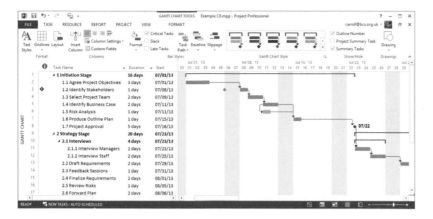

2 To change the color (and any other details) of the critical task bars, select the down arrow beneath Format on the Gantt chart Format ribbon. Select Bar Styles from the drop down menu to open the Bar Styles dialog box, scroll down to select critical tasks and make any changes

Task Path

In Project 2013 a further option for highlighting task paths has been introduced:

1 On the Gantt chart Format ribbon click Task Path and select from the link options:

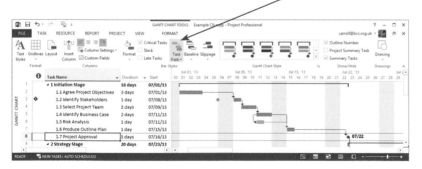

In the illustration above predecessors and driven predecessors for the Project Approval milestone were selected. Predecessors (non-critical tasks) are displayed in pale yellow and driven predecessors (critical tasks) are displayed in darker yellow. The other two display options are to select successor and driven successors and there is a final option to remove all highlighting.

Splitting Tasks

Normally, a task will be worked on from start to finish. But you can split a task if it needs to be interrupted and finished at a later time. Suppose that we have a task to Interview Managers and it needs to be split, as half of the managers are going to be on a conference the week it has been scheduled.

1 With your project in Gantt Chart view, click on Split Task on the Task ribbon and a pop-up asks you to select the split point

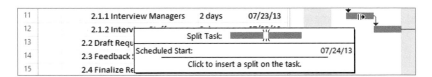

2 Position the pointer on the task bar where you want to make the split (the pop-up will show the date where the split will start, as in the example above) and click. The task will then be split, with a 1 day gap

3 You can now drag the right-hand part of the task bar, on the Gantt chart, to the right, to increase the gap (note that the cursor turns into a four-headed arrow, illustrated below, indicating that you can drag the task)

4 To remove a split, just drag the right-hand piece of the task bar back, so that it joins the left-hand piece again

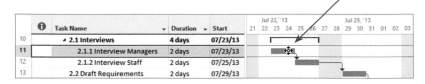

Moving Linked Tasks

In the previous topic, we dragged part of a split task to move it backwards or forward in time. We can do the same thing with any task, but, if the task is linked, it may cause a scheduling conflict. In the following example, we will move the task after the split task back, to use the available time.

		Task Name	Duration	Start	Jul 22, '13 / Jul 29, '13
10		⊿ 2.1 Interviews	7 days	07/23/13	
11		2.1.1 Interview Managers	2 days	07/23/13	
12		2.1.2 Interview Staff	2 days	07/30/13	
13		2.2 Draft Requirements	2 days	08/01/13	

1 Position your cursor over the task bar of the task you want to move (the cursor will turn into a 4-headed arrow), then drag the task bar back to where you want it to start and release the mouse key

2 If a Planning Wizard appears (as illustrated right), select "Remove the link" and click OK. The task will be unlinked and moved to where you dragged it (Cancel will undo the move)

3 Re-link the tasks as appropriate. In the example below, the moved task 2.1.2 stayed linked to the following task 2.2, so the preceding task 2.1.1 (which had lost its link in step 2) has also been linked to the following task 2.2

		Task Name	Duration	Start	Jul 22, '13 / Jul 29, '13
10		⊿ 2.1 Interviews	5 days	07/23/13	
11		2.1.1 Interview Managers	2 days	07/23/13	
12	▦	2.1.2 Interview Staff	2 days	07/24/13	
13		2.2 Draft Requirements	2 days	07/30/13	
14		2.3 Feedback Sessions	1 day	08/01/13	

Note that, in the example above, the moved task is no longer on the critical path, so it has turned blue. There is also a calendar symbol in the task information box. If you position your cursor over the calendar symbol, it will display a note that the task has a 'start no earlier than' constraint.

Constraints are covered in Chapter 11.

Summary

- Lag time and lead time are used to create gaps (lag time) and overlaps (lead time) between tasks. The lag or lead time is indicated by the length of the line linking the two tasks on the Gantt chart

- Task Inspector allows you to view the constraints, dependencies and calendars that impact a task's start date, and you can follow these links to investigate any issues

- Notes can be attached to any task and are indicated by a note symbol in the task's information box. They can be read, amended and deleted by double-clicking the note symbol or by double-clicking the task name and selecting the Note tab

- Deadline dates can be attached to any task that has a deadline. While they do not affect the scheduling, they will trigger a warning in the task information box if the task slips and is going to miss the deadline

- Moving around the Gantt chart can be done using the scroll bars, but the Scroll To Task function provides a useful shortcut for getting a task's task bar into view

- Another useful shortcut is Ctrl + Home, which will move to the top left-hand corner of the task sheet

- A critical task is one that will, if delayed, delay the final completion of the project. The critical path is the path through the project that links all the critical tasks

- Critical Tasks is the function, in Project, that is used for setting (or removing) the critical path

- Task Path is a new function that allows predecessor and successor tasks to be highlighted for a selected task

- Splitting a task allows the task to be split into two (or more) sections, with gaps of any required duration between them

- Tasks can be moved by dragging their task bar on the Gantt chart. If the task is linked, however, this may lead to a scheduling conflict. The best way to deal with this is to remove the link causing the conflict, move the task and then re-link it as required

7 Resources

Up to now we have dealt with planning a project and defining the tasks needed to carry it out. This chapter introduces project resources and the allocation of work to them.

Resource Sheet

Resources represent the human (people), material and financial resources you will use on your project. Resource Sheet view is where you enter details of these resources. It is called a sheet as it functions in a similar way to a spreadsheet. It can be accessed by selecting Resource Sheet on the View ribbon, or from the drop-down list of built in views from the Task ribbon.

 To enter a person, click in a blank Resource Name field, input the name of the resource and hit the Enter key

The Type defaults to Work (human resource), the Max Units to 100% (the full resource available to the project) and the Base Calendar to Standard. Costs are dealt with in the next chapter and, initially, it is best to leave these defaults as they are.

2 Add the person's Initials, and Group, if required, and then add in the other people resources, as in the following example

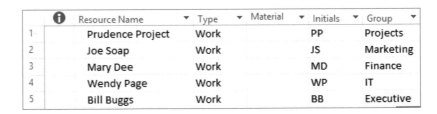

	Resource Name	Type	Material	Initials	Group
1	Prudence Project	Work		PP	Projects
2	Joe Soap	Work		JS	Marketing
3	Mary Dee	Work		MD	Finance
4	Wendy Page	Work		WP	IT
5	Bill Buggs	Work		BB	Executive

You can change any details by selecting the field and editing it. You can add new resources to the end of the resource sheet or insert new resources in the middle (click on the resource you wish to insert the new resource in front of and press the Insert key).

You can also delete a resource by clicking on the Resource ID (the number on the left-hand side of the sheet) and pressing Delete.

Resource Information

In addition to inputting information into the Resource Sheet, you can add additional resource information through the Resource Information dialog box.

1 In Resource Sheet view, select the name of the resource you wish to add additional information for and click Information, from the Resource ribbon, to open the Resource Information dialog box, as illustrated below

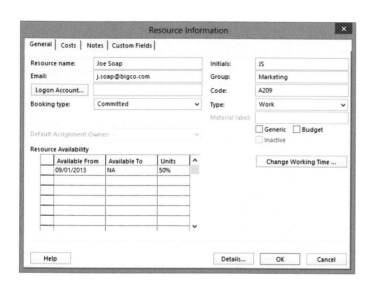

2 On the General tab, you can change any of the information you input to the Resource Sheet and also add information about email address' and availability

In the example above, Joe is not going to be available for the project until September and he will then only be available for 50% of the time.

The other fields on the General tab are Logon Account (to look up someone on your network); Booking Type (Committed or Proposed, if someone is only provisionally allocated); Generic (for a resource type where there may be a team of people providing the work); Budget (for financial resources); Change Working Time (access to their calendar); and Details (to look up their details from your Outlook address book). The use of these fields, where relevant, are dealt with in later topics.

Material and Cost Resources

In addition to work resources (people), you can also put in material resources (for consumable materials or supplies) and cost resources (where the cost is not dependant on the work or duration of a task).

 Open your project in Resource Sheet view and add in any material resources you will be using

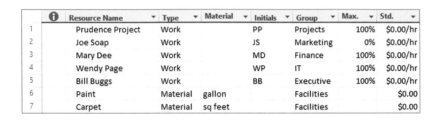

	ℹ	Resource Name ▾	Type ▾	Material ▾	Initials ▾	Group ▾	Max. ▾	Std. ▾
1		Prudence Project	Work		PP	Projects	100%	$0.00/hr
2		Joe Soap	Work		JS	Marketing	0%	$0.00/hr
3		Mary Dee	Work		MD	Finance	100%	$0.00/hr
4		Wendy Page	Work		WP	IT	100%	$0.00/hr
5		Bill Buggs	Work		BB	Executive	100%	$0.00/hr
6		Paint	Material	gallon		Facilities		$0.00
7		Carpet	Material	sq feet		Facilities		$0.00

Note that, in the above illustration, Joe Soap has 0% Max units. This is the result of changing his availability in the previous topic. It will show 0% until September, then it will show 50%.

2 Select a material resource and click on the Resource Information function on the Resource ribbon (note that, on the General tab, the work-related fields are deselected as they do not apply to material resources)

3 Select the Costs tab and input the cost: Standard Rate (used where the cost is dependant on the quantity used) and Per Use Cost (a one-off cost for using the resource)

Cost Resources

Cost resources are the third type of resource and they are used for costs that are unrelated to the work effort or the duration of a task. This would typically be for costs like travel or expenses that could be applied to a number of different tasks. Cost resources are dealt with in the next chapter.

Resource Notes

Resource notes can be attached to resources in a similar manner to attaching task notes to tasks.

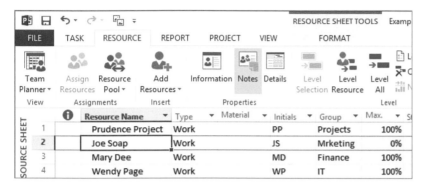

1 Select the Resource Name of the resource you want to attach the note to, click Notes on the Resource ribbon and the Resource Information dialog box opens at the Note tab (as illustrated)

2 Type in your note, format it if required and click OK. The resource sheet now shows a note symbol in the resource information box, as illustrated below

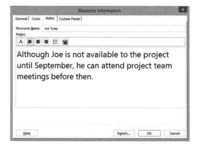

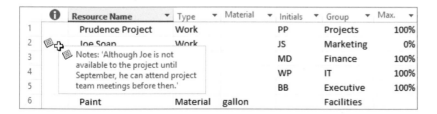

3 Position your cursor over the note symbol to display the note, as illustrated above

The note can be edited by double-clicking on it and making any required changes. It can be deleted by double-clicking on it and deleting all the text. It can also be accessed by opening the Resource Information dialog box and selecting the Notes tab.

Assigning Resources

Assigning resources is the process of allocating people and other resources to tasks so that they can be carried out.

1 In Gantt Chart view, select the task you wish to assign a resource to and click Assign Resources on the Resource ribbon (or press Alt + F10)

2 When the Assign Resources dialog box opens, select the Resource Name of the resource you wish to assign to the task and then click the Assign button

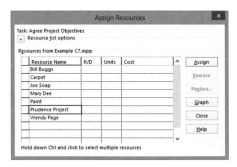

3 You can check a resource availability by selecting their name and clicking on the Graph button, which will display their work load as a graph in another pane below the Gantt chart

Once resources have been assigned to tasks, the Gantt chart will display the names of the resources allocated to each task, as in the illustration below. Where resources have been allocated at 100% (the default), no percentage is shown on the Gantt chart. But, if any resource is allocated at any other percentage, it is displayed after their name (as illustrated on task 1.3 below).

Hot tip

In order to create a work overload for some later topics, Calculate Project (explained in Chapter 11) has been turned off.

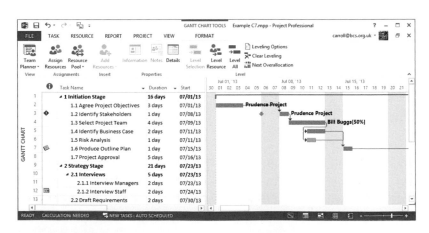

Multiple Resources

In many cases, you will just be assigning a single resource to each task (which is the best way of controlling a project). However, sometimes you may need to assign two or more resources to tasks.

1 Select the task you want to assign multiple resources to and then click Assign Resources on the Resource ribbon

2 Select the first resource name in the Assign Resources dialog box and click the Assign button (the resource will be assigned as in the previous topic)

3 Now select and assign the second resource

	ⓘ	Task Name	Duration	Start	Jul 01, '13	Jul 08, '13	Jul 15, '13
1		⊿ 1 Initiation Stage	16 days	07/01/13			
2		1.1 Agree Project Objectives	3 days	07/01/13	Prudence Project		
3	◆	1.2 Identify Stakeholders	1 day	07/08/13		Prudence Project	
4	⊕	1.3 Select Project Team	2 days	07/09/13		Bill Buggs[50%],Prudence Project	
5		1.4 Identify Business Case	2 days	07/11/13			
6		1.5 Risk Analysis	1 day	07/11/13			
7		1.6 Produce Outline Plan	1 day	07/15/13			

Both resources are now allocated to the task, but note that a warning symbol has been placed in the task information box. When we added the second resource, Project needs to know how we want this interpreted.

4 Click on the warning symbol to display the options, as illustrated below

	You added resources to this task. Do you want to:
○	Reduce duration but keep the same amount of work.
◉	Increase the amount of work but keep the same duration.
○	Reduce the hours resources work per day (units), but keep the same duration and work.

5 Select the first option to reduce the task duration, the second to keep the original duration or the third option to reduce the hours each will work

Selecting the second option (as above) will retain the duration of the task (two days) but increase the work effort to the sum of the two resources. In the example above this would be three days (as one resource is allocated at 50% and the other at 100%).

Hot tip

Hold down the Ctrl key in the Assign Resources dialog box to select more than one resource at one time.

87

Team Planner

Don't forget

Team Planner is only available in Project Professional, not in Project Standard.

Team Planner is a resource assignment view that was introduced in Project Professional 2010. It provides a drag and drop facility to simplify the assignment of tasks to resources, and the changes of assignments between resources.

1 Select Team Planner from the Resource ribbon or from the drop down list of built in views

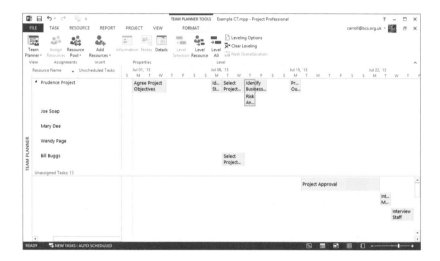

The upper part of the view displays the project resources with the tasks assigned to them. Overallocated resources are highlighted in red. Any allocated but unscheduled tasks will be displayed on the left. The lower part of the view displays the unassigned tasks.

2 Hover over a task to display the task level details, as illustrated on the right

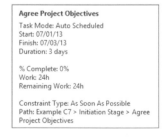

Agree Project Objectives
Task Mode: Auto Scheduled
Start: 07/01/13
Finish: 07/03/13
Duration: 3 days

% Complete: 0%
Work: 24h
Remaining Work: 24h

Constraint Type: As Soon As Possible
Path: Example C7 > Initiation Stage > Agree Project Objectives

3 Double click on a task to open the Task Information dialog box, or on a resource to open the Resource Information dialog box

4 Select Details on the Resource ribbon to split the view and display a resource form in the bottom of the view, as illustrated at the top of the page opposite

The resource form displays all the tasks allocated to the selected resource, as illustrated above.

5 To reallocate a task, simply drag it from its existing resource line and drop it onto the resource you wish to assign it to

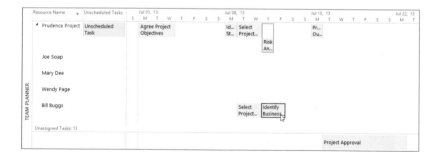

In the illustration above, a task has been dragged from the location highlighted in red in the top resource and dropped into the bottom resource. If this reassignment causes any conflicts, Project will display warnings and advice on the options for resolving them. Unallocated tasks (in the lower half of the screen) can be assigned in a similar manner:

6 Drag any unassigned tasks from the lower part of the team planner and drop them onto the required resource in the upper part of the team planner

Timeline

Timeline provides a simple to use, high-level, graphic display of the project timeline. The timeline can be copied to an email or any other office document.

1 To display the timeline in Gantt Chart view, select Timeline on the View ribbon

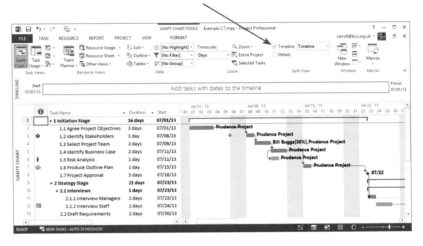

2 You can now specify the details you want displayed on the timeline, using Existing Tasks on the Format ribbon

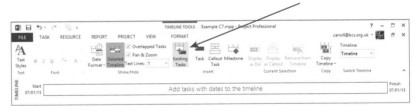

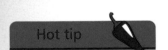

Hot tip

Click in the Timeline to make it active if the Gantt chart is active.

3 Select the detail required from the dialog box (for this example, the project stages have been selected)

4 Click OK to update the timeline with the selected details, as illustrated below

Formatting the Timeline

The Timeline Format ribbon contains functions for changing text styles and fonts, together with other formatting functions:

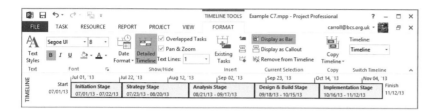

1 To improve the look of the timeline above, we can select each stage in turn and give it a different background color and appropriate text color, using the font group functions as illustrated below

2 Use the Text Styles function to change the overall look of the text and annotations

3 Use Add Existing Task from the Format ribbon to add an existing milestone (as illustrated below)

4 Insert new tasks, new milestones or new call out tasks (as illustrated below), using the other functions from the Format ribbon

5 Use Copy Timeline from the Format ribbon to copy to email or other office application

Summary

- Project resources represent the people or human resources (Work), material resources (Material) and financial resources (Cost) you will use on your project

- Resource Sheet view is the best place to input the basic details for your people and other project resources

- The Resource Information dialog box allows you to edit and add further resource information, including availability and working time

- Material resources can be used to allocate facilities and materials to the project, together with their costs. Material costs can be per unit costs or per use costs

- Cost resources can be used to record costs that are unrelated to the work effort or duration of a task. They are typically used for travel and other expenses

- Notes can be added to any resource and show up as a note symbol in the resource information box. Notes can be edited or deleted by double-clicking the note symbol

- Resources are assigned to tasks in Gantt Chart view, using the Assign Resources function on the Resource ribbon. Once assigned, they will be displayed on the Gantt chart

- Multiple resources can be assigned to a task and you can then select whether Project should reduce the duration of the task, increase the work effort or reduce the hours worked on the task

- Team Planner (only available in Project Professional) allows you to view assigned and unassigned tasks by resource, and allocate and re-allocate work between resources using the drag and drop functionality

- Timeline provides a simple to use, high-level, graphic display of your project timeline, which can be edited to show any required level of detail

- Project timelines can also be formatted and copied to email or any other office application for communication purposes, and they can be edited further in those applications

8 Project Costs

This chapter looks at adding revenue and fixed cost information to resources, tasks and assignments in order to build up the project budget.

Project Costs

Project costs fall into the general headings of: internal people costs, external people costs, other project costs and capital costs. All of these can be dealt with in Project. The ongoing revenue costs of operating the results of the project are not normally treated as project costs.

Project treats costs under two headings: Resource Costs (costs related to the people, material or cost resources you will use on the project) and Fixed Costs (not related to resource usage).

Resource Costs

Once you have identified all the stages, tasks and subtasks for a project, you will have estimated the work effort required to carry out the project. This should include the appropriate element of contingency (to deal with the unknown), based on where you are in the project. By adding resource costs for all the internal people who will be working on the project, Project will calculate all the people-related costs for you. Then you need to identify any external people costs (such as consultants, auditors, etc.) and feed those in as well.

When you have dealt with all the people related costs, then identify any material resource costs if your project is using costed material (such as paint or other types of consumables). Finally, any cost resources, which would cover travel, accommodation, training or other similar costs.

Fixed Costs

Once you have the internal and external people and material resource costs, you then need to identify any internal non-staff costs, such as any one-off charges for the use of facilities, rooms, computer usage, etc.

Finally, you will need to identify any other external capital or revenue costs, such as software package purchase, software development, equipment purchase or lease costs, and any other items of external expenditure.

All of these costs can be input into Project as Resource Costs or Fixed Costs on an appropriate task.

We will now work through each of these cost types and use the remaining topics in this chapter to see how they are treated in Project.

Resource Costs

Costs can be applied to resources or tasks and, typically, you will use resource costs for people on the project. Resource costs are normally shown as an hourly rate, which represents their salary plus overheads (that is their real cost to the business). Your organization may do things differently, so follow whatever their procedure is to calculate the appropriate hourly rates. The easiest way to allocate costs to resources is in the Resource Sheet.

1 Open the Resource Sheet by selecting Resource Sheet from the View ribbon

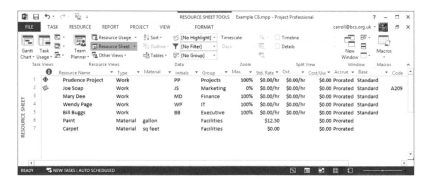

If any resources are highlighted in red it indicates a resource conflict (this is dealt with in Chapter 11).

2 Enter the appropriate hourly standard rate (and overtime rate if appropriate) for each resource, as illustrated below

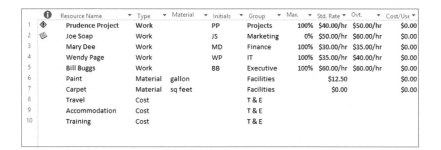

3 If a resource has a one-off cost for each use (such as hire of a meeting room), enter the cost in the Cost/Use field

4 Finally, there is also a resource type of Cost (used for travel, accommodation and training in the above example), which can be used to assign arbitrary costs to tasks, so the actual amount will need to be entered for each usage

Cost resources are fully explained later in this chapter (see page 100).

Fixed Costs

Fixed costs are used when a task has a fixed cost associated with it, rather than the cost being associated with the resource. In the following example, we are going to add the cost of purchasing a computer software package to the task Purchase Software.

 In Gantt Chart view, select Tables from the View ribbon and then select Cost from the drop down built in menu (as illustrated on the right)

The cost columns will be added to the task table, replacing the previous task Entry columns (as illustrated below). Note: you will need to move the divider between the table and Gantt chart to see all the table fields

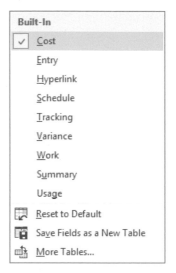

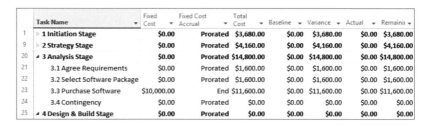

	Task Name	Fixed Cost	Fixed Cost Accrual	Total Cost	Baseline	Variance	Actual	Remaining
1	▷ 1 Initiation Stage	$0.00	Prorated	$3,680.00	$0.00	$3,680.00	$0.00	$3,680.00
9	▷ 2 Strategy Stage	$0.00	Prorated	$4,160.00	$0.00	$4,160.00	$0.00	$4,160.00
20	▲ 3 Analysis Stage	$0.00	Prorated	$14,800.00	$0.00	$14,800.00	$0.00	$14,800.00
21	3.1 Agree Requirements	$0.00	Prorated	$1,600.00	$0.00	$1,600.00	$0.00	$1,600.00
22	3.2 Select Software Package	$0.00	Prorated	$1,600.00	$0.00	$1,600.00	$0.00	$1,600.00
23	3.3 Purchase Software	$10,000.00	End	$11,600.00	$0.00	$11,600.00	$0.00	$11,600.00
24	3.4 Contingency	$0.00	Prorated	$0.00	$0.00	$0.00	$0.00	$0.00
25	▲ 4 Design & Build Stage	$0.00	Prorated	$0.00	$0.00	$0.00	$0.00	$0.00

 Type the estimated fixed cost for the task into the Fixed Cost field, as illustrated above

In this example, we have entered $10,000 as the estimated fixed cost. There is also a resource allocated to the task and, therefore, the total cost of the task includes the fixed cost plus the resource cost. The task is estimated at 5 days (40 hours) at a standard rate of $40 per hour making $1,600 so the total cost for the task is $11,600 as illustrated above.

The other fields in the cost table are the fixed cost accrual method (we have selected to accrue the cost at the end of the task), then baseline, variance, actual and remaining.

Variable Resource Costs

It is quite possible that resource costs may change during the course of a project. For example, someone may receive a promotion or salary increase for doing such a good job on the project. Any changes to resource costs should be entered using the Resource Information dialog box.

1 In Resource Sheet view, select the Resource Name of the resource to be changed, click Information on the Resource ribbon to open the Resource Information dialog box and select the Costs tab

Don't forget

You can also double-click on the Resource Name to open the Resource Information dialog box.

2 On the A (Default) tab, click in the next available Effective Date (below any existing cost information) and use the drop-down arrow to select the date for the new rate

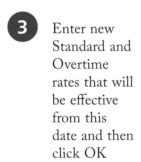

3 Enter new Standard and Overtime rates that will be effective from this date and then click OK

Hot tip

You can also put in a percentage figure for an increase or a negative percentage for a decrease.

These new cost rates will become effective on all work from the effective date onwards. All work before that effective date will still be costed at the existing rate. If required, you can input up to 24 changes of resource costs for each resource.

Cost Rate Tables

In addition to being able to change cost rates, Project will also allow you to set up tables of rates for a resource. This can be useful if you need to use different cost rates for different types of work for the same person.

The cost rate tables are selected in the Costs tab in the Resource Information dialog box.

1 In Resource Sheet view, double-click on a Resource Name to open the Resource Information dialog box

2 Select the Costs tab at the top and then click on tab B in the middle Cost rate tables area, as illustrated

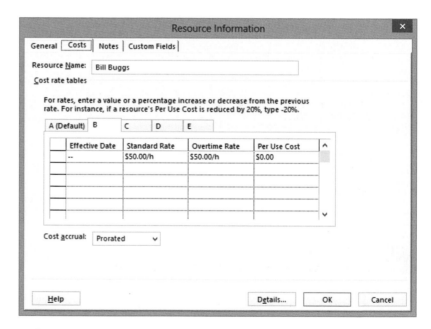

3 Type in the second standard rate (and overtime rate if it is required)

4 Enter the effective date, if relevant (see previous topic)

5 Add any further rates in tabs C, D and E, if required

6 Click OK to save the new rates table

Applying Resource Rates

Having set up a cost rates table, as in the previous topic, it can now be applied to any relevant tasks where this resource is allocated. Rate A will be used by default unless it is changed.

1 Select Task Usage from the View ribbon

	❶	Task Name	Work	Details	Jul 08, '13 M	T	W	T	F	S
2		⊿ Agree Project Objectives	24 hrs	Work						
		Prudence Project	24 hrs	Work						
3	◆	⊿ Identify Stakeholders	8 hrs	Work	8h					
		Prudence Project	8 hrs	Work	8h					
4		⊿ Select Project Team	24 hrs	Work			12h	12h		
		Prudence Project	16 hrs	Work			8h	8h		
		Bill Buggs	8 hrs	Work			4h	4h		
5	ⓘ	⊿ Identify Business Case	16 hrs	Work					8h	8h

2 Identify the resource and task where you wish to apply a different rate and double-click on the Resource Name to open the Assignment Information dialog box

3 On the General tab, click on the down-arrow beside the Cost rate table to show the drop-down list of rates, as illustrated right

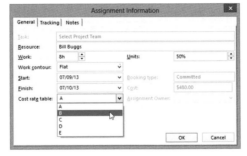

4 Select the relevant rate you wish to apply to this task and click OK

Note that, in the example above, the new cost rate has now been applied and the cost of the work on this task has been recalculated at the new rate. This has reduced the rate from $60 to $50 per hour, so the cost of the 8 hours of work on this task has reduced from $480 to $400. Apply the Cost table to see this:

	Task Name	Fixed Cost	Fixed Cost Accrual	Total Cost	Details	T	W	T	F	S
	Prudence Project			$320.00	Work					
4	⊿ Select Project Team	$0.00	Prorated	$1,040.00	Work	12h	12h			
	Prudence Project			$640.00	Work	8h	8h			
	Bill Buggs			$400.00	Work	4h	4h			
5	⊿ Identify Business Case	$0.00	Prorated	$640.00	Work				8h	8h
	Prudence Project			$640.00	Work				8h	8h
6	⊿ Risk Analysis	$0.00	Prorated	$320.00	Work				8h	
	Prudence Project			$320.00	Work				8h	

Don't forget

Applying the Cost table from the View ribbon was covered on page 96.

Cost Resources

In addition to work (human) resources and material resources, there are also cost resources. These are used for types of costs other than fixed or capital costs. They are typically used for travel, accommodation and training costs. To use these cost resources, we first need to set them up in the Resource Sheet.

1 Open the Resource Sheet by selecting Resource Sheet from the View ribbon

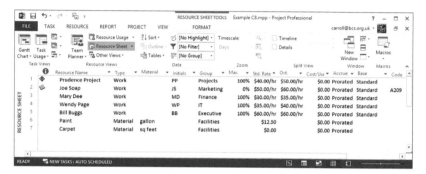

2 Select a blank line and enter a name for the cost resource, as illustrated below

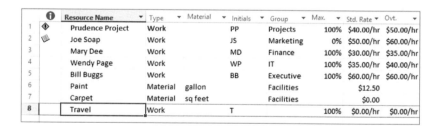

Note that Project automatically completes the default type, initials, max, charge rates and other information. This now needs to be changed:

3 Move to the resource type column and type Cost or select it from the drop down list

...cont'd

Note that, in the previous illustration, once cost is selected as the resource type, several of the automatically completed fields are now cleared. In particular, the cost fields are blanked out. This is because we will be allocating the cost each time we use this resource.

4 Add in any further information and other cost resources, as in the following illustration

	ⓘ	Resource Name	Type	Material	Initials	Group	Max.	Std.	Ovt.	Cost/Use
8		Travel	Cost			T & E				
9		Accommodation	Cost			T & E				
10		Training	Cost			T & E				

Using Cost Resources

Cost resources are allocated to tasks in a similar way to work and material resources:

1 In Gantt Chart view, select the task you wish to apply a cost resource to

	ⓘ	Task Name	Duration	Start	Jul 22, '13 / Jul 29, '13 / Aug 05, '13
9		⊿ 2 Strategy Stage	21 days	07/23/13	
10		⊿ 2.1 Interviews	5 days	07/23/13	
11		2.1.1 Interview Managers	2 days	07/23/13	Prudence Project
12	📅	2.1.2 Interview Staff	2 days	07/24/13	Prudence Project

2 Select Assign Resources from the Resource ribbon to open the Assign Resources dialog box as illustrated below

3 Select the required cost resource, click Assign and then enter the budget cost for this task ($200 in the example). The cost resource and budget are then displayed on the Gantt chart, as illustrated below

	ⓘ	Task Name	Duration	Start	Jul 22, '13 / Jul 29, '13 / Aug 05, '13
9		⊿ 2 Strategy Stage	21 days	07/23/13	
10		⊿ 2.1 Interviews	5 days	07/23/13	
11		2.1.1 Interview Managers	2 days	07/23/13	Prudence Project, Travel[$200.00]
12	📅	2.1.2 Interview Staff	2 days	07/24/13	Prudence Project
13		2.2 Draft Requirements	2 days	07/30/13	Prudence Project

Summary

- Project can track budget and actual costs for internal and external people, material and other revenue cost items, together with capital costs

- Project differentiates between resource costs (costs associated with people, material or other cost resources) and fixed costs (such as equipment purchase) that are not resource-related

- Resource sheet is used for entering details of human resources (people), including standard and overtime hourly costs rates

- Details of material resource can also be entered in the resource sheet, with quantity costs or per use costs

- Details of cost resource can also be entered in the resource sheet, but, in their case, no cost details are entered as these are input when the resource is allocated to a task

- Fixed costs for capital or other fixed cost items can be input in Gantt Chart view by applying the Cost table to the view in place of the normal entry table

- Resource cost can be varied through the life of the project, to reflect changes in salary, for example, by using the Costs tab in the Resource Information dialog box

- In addition to the default cost rate, four additional cost rates can be specified, if a resource is to be charged differently for different types of work. Again, these rates can be varied through the life of the project

- These additional (non-default) resource rates are best applied in the Task Usage view, using the Assignment Information dialog box

- Cost resources are set up in the Resource Sheet, as for other resource types, but no costs are entered for them

- When required, cost resources can be applied to a task using the Assign Resources dialog box and then the relevant amount can be entered in the dialog box

9 Project Calendars

This chapter explains what the various calendars are, how to set them up and assign and change them for individual resources and time-critical tasks.

Calendars

The scheduling process consists of allocating tasks to resources, in line with their availability. So, the first step in scheduling is to know the availability and non-availability of the resources you will be using (e.g. when they are going to be on vacation, training or any other absences during the project).

Project uses calendars to determine working and non-working days, default start time and the working hours in a day. Calendars are automatically assigned to each work resource (person), but they can also be applied to tasks. So resources, tasks and calendars are all interlinked.

Tasks

Tasks determine the amount of work that needs to be carried out (the work effort), expressed as the total number of person/hours that need to be worked to complete the task. Until any resources are assigned to the task, Project assumes that a single resource (100%) will be allocated to it and schedules it on that basis.

Resources

Once a resource is allocated to a task, Project recalculates the duration (how many days it will take to complete), based on the amount of available resources allocated to it.

Calendars

Project then checks the resource calendar for each resource's availability and, if necessary, reschedules the task to take into account the availability of the resource. Finally, Project checks if a task calendar has been assigned to a task and, if so, also takes that into account when scheduling the task.

There are three types of calendar: base calendars, resource calendars and task calendars. Base calendars define the working days and hours for the whole project (or for a group of resources within the project). Resource calendars define the working days and working hours for each individual resource (person). Task calendars define when a task can or cannot take place.

The Standard calendar is the default project base calendar. It defines the working days and hours for the project. When a resource is added to a project, the standard calendar is allocated to that resource as its base calendar. Any changes to the standard calendar will be reflected in the dependant resource calendars.

There is a third element to this relationship, and that is the project defaults. These form the top-level of the relationship:

1 Project Defaults are set under Schedule in the Project Options dialog box (illustrated below). This allows you to change the default working hours and hours in a working day, week and month. These are all used by Project in setting task durations and scheduling tasks

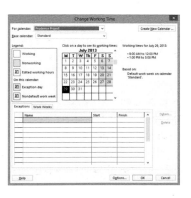

Beware

Making any changes to these defaults can have a significant impact on your project schedule. This is covered in the next topic.

105

2 Base Calendars (as illustrated right) are based on the project defaults, but you can redefine the working hours in a day and in a week for the project. More importantly, you can also set any non-working days, such as public holidays

3 Resource Calendars are created for each resource and inherit their base calendar working days and hours. They are used to set annual vacation and other non working time. Task calendars are similar and can be created for any task that requires one

Project Defaults

Project defaults are initially set so that working time is Monday to Friday, 8:00 AM to 12:00 PM and 1:00 PM to 5:00 PM. The standard calendar (see next topic) is also initially set to these working days and times.

Changing the defaults will change the way tasks are allocated, their duration and the way that resources are allocated to them. If you change the project defaults, it does not automatically change the standard calendar or any calendars based on it. So, if you do make changes to the defaults, you may also need to make changes to all your other calendars.

Beware

Even if you don't work these hours, don't change the defaults unless you absolutely have to. It can make scheduling a real nightmare.

1 Select Options from the File tab to open the Program Options dialog box

2 Select Schedule from the menu on the left hand side (as illustrated below) to access the schedule options

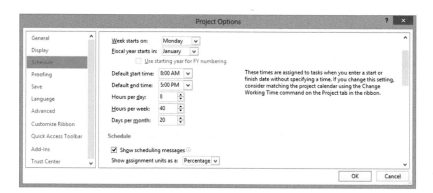

3 Make any changes required to the project defaults

4 If you want the changes to apply to all new projects, click the drop down arrow beside your project name and select All New Projects, then click OK

Beware

If you change the Default hours per day after you have entered any tasks, the task durations will change, as they will still have the original hours as their work effort.

5 If you have made any changes to the Default start time, Default end time, Hours per day or Hours per week, you will need to change the Standard calendar (and any other base calendars you have created) to bring them into line with the new defaults (see next topic)

Standard Calendar

The standard calendar has the default working time set as 8:00 AM to 12:00 PM and 1:00 PM to 5:00 PM on Monday to Friday. If you have changed the project defaults, you will need to bring the standard calendar into line. You can then put in any public or other holidays that will apply to the whole project.

1 Select Change Working Time from Project ribbon to open the Change Working Time dialog box

2 The scroll bar on the right of the calendar changes the month. Click on a day to show its working time

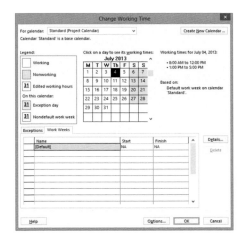

3 To change all working times, select the Work Weeks tab, select Default and click the Details button

4 In the Details dialog box (not illustrated), select the days to change (Monday to Friday for the whole week), change the From and To times as required and then click OK

5 To enter holidays, select the required month and day, click the Exceptions tab, enter the holiday name and click the Details button

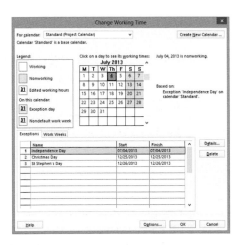

6 In the Details dialog box, make the day non-working and click OK to save it

New Base Calendar

Project comes with three base calendars (standard, night shift and 24 hours) but, if none of these are suitable, you can create a new one from the project defaults or by copying an existing calendar.

1 Select Change Working Time from the Project ribbon and click Create New Calendar (top right-hand corner)

2 Name the new calendar and select if you want to start with a copy of an existing calendar

The new calendar will open in the Change Working Time dialog box and will inherit anything from the calendar you based it on.

3 Select the Work Weeks tab, select Default, click on the Details button to open the Details dialog box and enter details of your required From and To working times, as illustrated

This example is for a shift, so Monday would need to be 9:00 PM to 12:00 AM and Saturday 12:00 AM to 5:00 AM.

Don't forget

In Project, 12:00 AM is midnight and 12:00 PM is midday. If you select the 24-hour clock, 00:00 is midnight and 12:00 is midday.

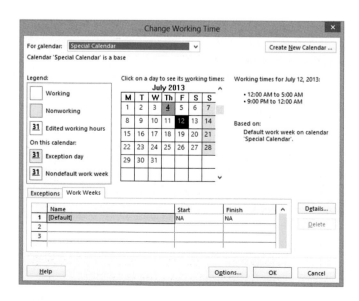

Assigning a Calendar

Having set up your standard calendar and created any new base calendars, you can now assign them to the project team, as required. The standard calendar is assigned by default, the other base calendars can be assigned using the Resource Information dialog box or directly in Resource Sheet view.

1 In Resource Sheet view, double-click on the Resource Name of the person whose base calendar you wish to change to open the Resource Information dialog box

2 On the General tab, click the Change Working Time button (on the right) to open the Change Working Time dialog box for the resource

3 Click the down arrow beside Base calendar to get the drop down list of calendars, select the required base calendar and click OK. Click OK again to close the Resource Information dialog box

Hot tip

If you have made changes to a resource calendar and then assign a new base calendar to the resource, the changes will be retained after the new base calendar has been applied.

4 To assign a new base calendar directly in Resource Sheet view, click on the existing Base Calendar (on the right-hand side of the sheet) and select the required calendar from the drop down list

The new base calendar is applied to the resource in exactly the same way as using the Resource Information dialog box.

Task Calendar

If a task can only take place at a certain time and/or on certain days, this can be defined by assigning a task calendar to the task.

For example, it may be that a presentation to management must take place at a weekly management meeting, and these are always held on Friday mornings.

1 If necessary, split the task into the report preparation and the presentation (to isolate the presentation)

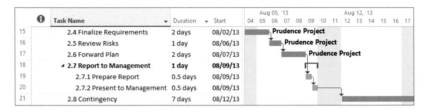

Don't forget

By making a copy of a standard calendar, it will inherit any holidays.

2 Create a new base Management Meeting calendar (as a copy of Standard) and click OK

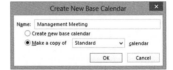

3 The Change Working Time dialog box will open at the new calendar. Select Default on the Work Weeks tab and click the Details button

4 Select Monday to Thursday on the left, then click on the Set days to the non-working time option on the right

5 Then select Friday on the left, Set days to specific times on the right, delete the afternoon From working time (this will also delete the afternoon To working time) to just leave Friday mornings as working time and then click OK twice to save this

...cont'd

We have now created a Management Meetings calendar with just Friday mornings as working time. We now have to assign it to the relevant task as a task calendar.

6 In Gantt Chart view, double-click on the Present to Management task to open the Task Information dialog box and select the Advanced tab, as illustrated below

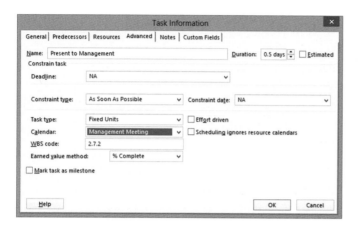

7 Assign the new calendar (as illustrated above) and the task is rescheduled to the next available Friday morning:

		Task Name	Duration	Start	
15		2.4 Finalize Requirements	2 days	08/05/13	Prudence Project
16		2.5 Review Risks	1 day	08/07/13	Prudence Project
17		2.6 Forward Plan	2 days	08/08/13	Prudence Project
18		2.7 Report to Management	4.5 days	08/12/13	
19		2.7.1 Prepare Report	0.5 days	08/12/13	
20		2.7.2 Present to Management	0.5 days	08/16/13	
21		2.8 Contingency	7 days	08/16/13	

As the delay to the presentation to management has effectively put a 3.5 day lag time between preparing the report and presenting it to management, the tasks in front of it are no longer on the critical path (note that they have turned blue). They can slip by 3.5 days without impacting the project. Of course, the end of the project has just been put back as well (unless there is spare lag time further on in the project).

One final point to note is that a task calendar symbol has now been created in the task's information box to warn us that this task has a calendar assigned to it.

Resource Calendar

Each resource is automatically assigned a resource calendar. This is initially based on the standard calendar, although a different base calendar can be assigned, if required. The resource calendar will inherit any holidays or project-wide variations, but it also needs to have resource-specific variations added, such as vacation or other non-working time and non-standard working hours.

Don't forget

Assigning a calendar was covered on page 109.

Change Working Hours

Individual resources may well have non-standard working hours or may work part-time. Both of these variations can be recorded in their resource calendar. Changes to working hours are entered through the Change Working Time dialog box.

1 Select Change Working Time from the Project ribbon to open the Change Working Time dialog box

2 At the top, select the resource you wish to change, select the Work Weeks tab and click the Details button on the right hand side to open the Details dialog box (see below right)

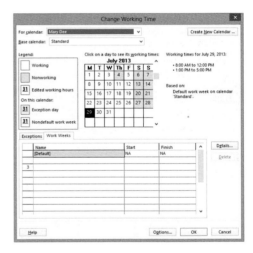

3 Select the days to change on the left and select "Set days to these specific working times"

4 Enter the new working hours for the resource and click OK

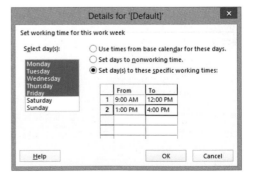

Change Working Week

The working week for a resource can also be changed in the Change Working Time dialog box. For example, if a resource now only works Monday to Thursday:

1 Open the Details for the resource and select Friday

2 Click "Set days to non-working time" option and click OK

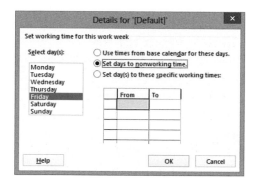

Vacations and Absences

Vacations and any other absences are also entered through Change Working Time.

1 Open the Change Working Time dialog box, select the resource for whom you wish to enter a vacation, or other absence, and click on the Exceptions tab (see below)

2 Click under Name on the Exception tab and enter a name for the absence

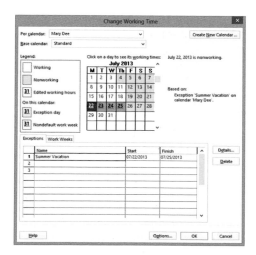

3 Select the Start and Finish dates using the drop down calendars in the Start and Finish columns

4 Enter any other absences, then click OK twice to save the changes and close the Resource Information dialog box

Summary

- When allocating a resource to a task and scheduling it, Project uses calendars to check the availability of that resource to carry out the task, and on any limitations on when the task can be performed

- Project defaults determine how Project will schedule work, base calendars are used to define project or group working times, while resource calendars are used to determine an individual resource's availability. Task calendars provide an option for determining when a time-critical task can be performed

- Project defaults specify the number of working hours in a day and a week, for scheduling purposes, and the default start and end time for a working day. They also define the first day of the week, the start of the fiscal year and the number of working days in a month

- The standard (project) calendar is the default base calendar for the project and is where project working time and non-working days are specified. It needs to be kept in step with the project defaults

- A new base calendar is best created based on the standard calendar, so that it inherits any project information

- The standard calendar is allocated to all resources by default, but any other base calendar can be allocated through the Change Working Time dialog box or on the Resource Sheet

- Task calendars are used when a task can only happen at certain times. They are defined by limiting the working time and then allocated to a task through the Task Information dialog box

- Resource calendars are used to enter non-standard working hours for a resource and to change the working week (days worked)

- Resource calendars are also used to set the non-working time for each individual resource, by defining their vacations, training and other non-available times

10 Project Scheduling

This chapter deals with scheduling a project, and how the different task types and contouring affect that process. It also covers setting and clearing baselines and interim plans.

User Controlled Scheduling

User controlled scheduling allows you to schedule tasks manually with whatever information you have available. It is the alternative mode to automatic scheduling, which will schedule tasks with calculated dates and durations. You can set either mode as the default and override the default for individual tasks.

1 To set the mode to manual scheduling, click on Mode on the Task ribbon and select Manually Schedule from the drop down list. All new tasks will now be manually scheduled, but existing tasks will be unaltered

2 To change an existing, automatically scheduled task to manually scheduled, select the task and click on Manually Schedule on the Task ribbon (to the left of Mode)

3 To create a manually scheduled task, click Insert Task on the Task ribbon while in manually scheduled mode

4 Enter the task name (as illustrated below)

	Task Name	Duration	Start	Sep 23, '13	Sep 30, '13
27	◢ 4 Design & Build Stage	20 days?	09/24/13		
28	4.1 Design Work				
29	4.2 Dummy Task	20 days	09/24/13		
30	◢ 5 Implementation Stage	20 days	10/22/13		

5 You can now manually schedule the task by entering a duration and start date when known

6 You can also enter placeholder text in the duration and start fields (as illustrated below)

	Task Name	Duration	Start	Sep 23, '13	Sep 30, '13
27	◢ 4 Design & Build Stage	20.5 days?	09/24/13		
28	4.1 Design Work	5 days	09/24/13		
29	4.2 Initial Build Work	n/a	October		
30	4.3 Dummy Task	20 days	09/24/13		
31	◢ 5 Implementation Stage	20 days	10/22/13		

Hot tip

Note that Project uses a different style Gantt bar (with shaded ends) for manually scheduled tasks.

Automatic Scheduling

For automatic scheduling, Project uses the tasks, the resources allocated to them and the resource and task calendars to work out when tasks can be started, worked on and completed.

Forward-Scheduling

The default approach to scheduling is to forward-schedule from a start date. You can also backward-schedule from a finish date, although there are certain problems that can result from this (covered later in this chapter).

The way that the schedule will be affected when resources, work effort or durations change is also dependent on the scheduling method and task types. The scheduling method can be either effort-driven or not. Tasks can be of fixed unit, fixed duration or fixed work types. The default is fixed unit, non-effort-driven tasks, but we will look at examples of each of these types.

Effort-Driven Scheduling

With effort-driven scheduling turned off, adding an additional resource to a 2-day duration, fixed unit task will increase the work effort by 2 days to 4 days, but the duration will remain unchanged (as there are now two people doing it).

This can be changed to effort-driven scheduling in Project Options on the File tab. With effort-driven scheduling on, the duration of a task is adjusted to fit in with any changes to the resources. If a task is going to require 16 hours work effort and you allocate two resources to it (at 100%), it will be given a duration of 8 hours (1 day).

If you then remove one of the resources, the additional day's work will be reallocated to the remaining resource, so the duration will be extended to 2 days.

Task Types

The task type (fixed unit, fixed duration or fixed work) will determine what will be changed to accommodate any other changes. The basic equation used by Project is:

$$\textbf{Work = Duration x Units}$$

Where Work is the work effort required, Duration is how long it will take and Units are resources and their allocation percentage.

Fixed Unit Tasks

The fixed unit task is the default task type in Project. If resources are added to or removed from a task, the work effort or duration will be affected. In the following example, we will allocate a second resource to a task.

1 In Gantt Chart view select Details from the View ribbon

2 In the above example, we have selected a 1-day task with a single resource assigned to it and 8 hours of work have been allocated to the resource in the (lower) task form

3 If we assign a second resource to the task (as illustrated below), the duration remains as 1 day with 8 hours work now allocated to each of the two resources

4 Click on the smart tag to change this, to reduce the duration to half a day with 4 hours work allocated to each of the resources, if that is what was required

Note that Effort driven is not selected in the Task From. If selected, the allocation of a second resource would reduce the duration rather than increase the work effort.

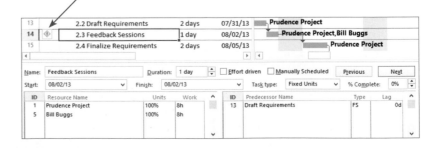

Fixed Duration Tasks

If a task is a fixed duration task, then (as the name implies) the duration remains fixed whether resources are added or removed. This has an impact on the way scheduling takes place, depending on whether effort-driven scheduling is being used or not.

Effort-Driven Scheduling

If effort-driven scheduling is being used, this means that adding another resource to an existing task will split the work between the two resources. The work effort will remain the same, the duration will remain the same, so their units will be reduced to 50% to balance that.

Non-Effort-Driven Scheduling

If effort-driven scheduling is not being used, this means that adding another resource to an existing task will double the work. The duration stays the same, the units will be 100%, so the work effort will double (an example of this follows).

1 Select a task with one resource allocated to it and, in the lower panel (Task Form), change the task type to Fixed Duration and deselect "Effort driven" if selected

2 Now, if a second resource is assigned to the task

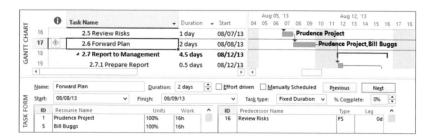

The duration has stayed the same so the work effort has doubled to 32 hours. This is the type of task to use when duration stays the same regardless of the number of resources allocated.

Fixed Work Tasks

The third type of task is the fixed work task. A fixed work task must be effort-driven (as the amount of work is fixed), so only the duration and resource units can be affected. Adding another resource will reduce the duration, while increasing the duration will reduce the resource units.

1 Select a task with one resource assigned to it and, in the lower panel (Task Form), change the "Task type" to Fixed Work (note that "Effort driven" deselects so it cannot be changed) and click OK

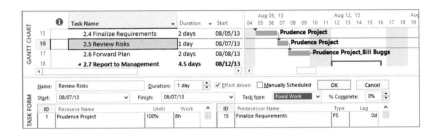

2 Now, if a second resource is assigned to the task (as below), the work effort remains 8 hours (4 hours each) so the duration has reduced to half a day

3 Change the Duration back to 1 day and a smart tag appears asking if you want to increase the work effort or decrease the hours worked by each resource (the default)

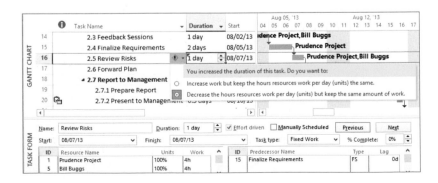

Resource Contouring

Project includes a feature that allows you to contour resource availability. This feature is aimed at situations where an individual is only available to a project part-time, with the percentage of their available time changing from period to period. Alternatively, it would be applicable if a team of people were going to be working on a task or set of tasks and the team were going to have varying numbers of people available over time (perhaps building up the team initially and then releasing them in a phased way).

1 In Resource Sheet view, select the resource you wish to contour and click Information on the Resource ribbon to open the Resource Information dialog box

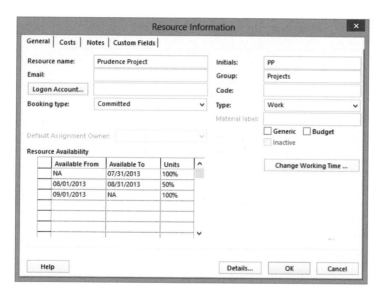

2 On the General tab, enter the Available From and To dates with the relevant Units (in the above example, the resource is only available 50% during August)

3 If this produces any conflicts with the scheduled work for this resource, the resource will be highlighted in red, with a warning symbol in the resource's information box (see below). Conflicts are dealt with in the next chapter

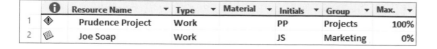

		Resource Name	Type	Material	Initials	Group	Max.
1	◈	Prudence Project	Work		PP	Projects	100%
2	📝	Joe Soap	Work		JS	Marketing	0%

Task Contouring

When you assign a resource to a task, the total work is spread evenly throughout the duration of the task. This is referred to as a flat contour, but there are a number of other contours that you can apply in Project.

Contours can be applied or changed in Task Usage or Resource Usage views. In the former, the resources are grouped by task; in the latter, tasks are grouped by resource. In both cases, the right-hand side of the screen displays the work values and is used to contour the work.

Contours are applied using the Assignment Information dialog box. There are eight preset contours available:

Flat
Work hours are distributed evenly through the task duration.

Back Loaded
The hours start low and ramp up towards the end of the task.

Front Loaded
The hours start at 100% at the start of the task and tail off towards the end.

Double Peak
The hours peak twice during the task duration.

Early Peak
The hours peak during the first quarter of the task duration.

Late Peak
The hours peak during the last quarter of the task duration.

Bell
The hours start and finish low and peak in the middle of the task duration.

Turtle
Similar to Bell, but the hours start and finish higher (i.e. there is less variation).

Once a contour has been applied to a task, any changes to the start or finish dates, the resources allocated or the duration will be applied using that contour.

Applying a Contour

To apply a contour in Resource Usage view (the process is exactly the same in Task Usage view):

1 Select a task that is at least 2 days long (contouring is only really practical on larger tasks)

		Resource Name	Work	Details	Jul 08, '13 M	T	W	T	F	S	S	Jul 15, '13 M	T	W
1		⊿ Prudence Project	328 hrs	Work		8h	8h	8h	16h				8h	8h
		Agree Project Objectives	24 hrs	Work										
		Identify Stakeholders	8 hrs	Work	8h									
		Select Project Team	16 hrs	Work			8h	8h						
		Identify Business Case	16 hrs	Work					8h				8h	
		Risk Analysis	8 hrs	Work					8h					
		Produce Outline Plan	8 hrs	Work										8h
		Interview Managers	16 hrs	Work										
		Interview Staff	16 hrs	Work										
		Draft Requirements	16 hrs	Work										

2 Double-click on the task name to open the Assignment Information dialog box and select the General tab, as illustrated

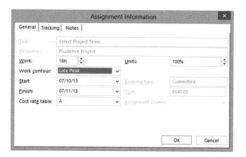

3 Click the down arrow beside Work contour, select the contour you wish to apply and then click OK (in the example above, Late Peak was selected)

		Resource Name	Work	Details		T	W	T	F	S	S	Jul 15, '13 M	T	W	T
1		⊿ Prudence Project	312 hrs	Work		8h	1.2h	3.6h	7.2h			4h	16h	8h	8h
		Agree Project Objectives	24 hrs	Work											
		Identify Stakeholders	8 hrs	Work		8h									
		Select Project Team	16 hrs	Work			1.2h	3.6h	7.2h			4h			
		Identify Business Case	16 hrs	Work									8h	8h	
		Risk Analysis	8 hrs	Work									8h		
		Produce Outline Plan	8 hrs	Work											8h
		Interview Managers	16 hrs	Work											
		Interview Staff	16 hrs	Work											
		Draft Requirements	16 hrs	Work											

The 16 hours work, in the example above, has now been contoured so that the hours build up slowly and peak late in the task. The larger the task, the more apparent the contouring. The late peak symbol has been inserted into the task's information box to indicate that a contour has been applied to the task.

Try applying the other contour types (as listed opposite) to see their effects on a task.

Setting a Baseline

Once you have created your project schedule, allocated resources, resolved any conflicts, and are happy with the project schedule, you are ready to set a baseline.

A baseline represents a record of a set point in time where you have agreed and fixed your project schedule. Project can hold up to eleven baselines for each project, named Baseline (for the first one) and then Baseline 1 to Baseline 10.

The first baseline you set should contain the original schedule only; subsequent baselines will contain the current schedule, with any actual data up to that point.

When you set a baseline, the dates, times and other data are recorded for all tasks.

1 In Gantt Chart view, select Set Baseline from the Project ribbon to open the Set Baseline dialog box (as illustrated right)

2 Select Set baseline and For: Entire project and click OK to save the baseline

Hot tip

Baselines 1 to 10 can also be selected in the Save Baseline dialog box, and previously saved baselines can be updated by saving them again.

3 Select Project Information from the Project ribbon to open the Project Information dialog box. Click the Statistics button to view the current, baseline and actual details for the project (as illustrated below)

Project Statistics for 'Example C10.mpp'

	Start	Finish
Current	07/01/13	11/19/13
Baseline	07/01/13	11/19/13
Actual	NA	NA
Variance	0d	0d

	Duration	Work	Cost
Current	100.5d?	348h	$25,128.00
Baseline	100.5d	348h	$25,128.00
Actual	0d	0h	$0.00
Remaining	100.5d?	348h	$25,128.00

Percent complete:

Duration: 0%   Work: 0%   Close

Interim Plans

As well as setting up to 11 baselines (which should be retained throughout the project), you can also create up to ten interim plans during the course of the project.

You may wish to create a new baseline at the end of each project stage, to reflect any changes to the project that have been agreed during that stage. But you may also wish to use interim plans to track more detailed changes to the project.

While a baseline saves a lot of information about a project, an interim plan just saves details of the current task start and end dates.

1   In Gantt Chart view, select Set Baseline from the Project ribbon to open the Set Baseline dialog box

2   Select Set interim plan, select Copy: Scheduled Start/Finish, select Into: Start 1/Finish 1, select For: Entire project and click OK

3   As the project progresses, you can copy into Start 2/Finish 2 and so on

4   You can also update any existing interim plans by copying new information over the information previously saved

5   If you want to save interim plans for just the current stage of the project, select the tasks in the Gantt chart before opening the Save Baseline dialog box, then select For: Selected tasks instead of For: Entire project in Step 2 (above)

Interim plans are very useful for tracking changes made during a project stage. Then, at the end stage review, you will be able to look back and see what was changed and when. They can also be used for tracking changes during the whole project and used as part of the end project review, but, in practice, baselines are probably more suitable for this.

Clearing a Baseline

As well as updating baselines and interim plans, you can also clear them for the whole project, or for selected tasks.

1 Select Set Baseline on the Project ribbon and then select Clear Baseline to open the Clear Baseline dialog box

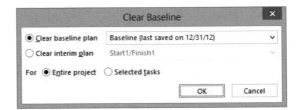

2 Select Clear baseline plan, select For: Entire project (as illustrated above) and click OK to clear the baseline

3 Select Project Information on the Project ribbon and click the Statistics button to confirm the baseline has gone

4 To clear selected tasks, first select the task names in Gantt Chart view

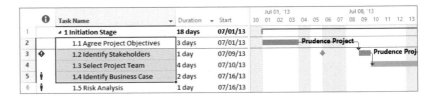

5 Select Set Baseline from the Project ribbon and then Clear Baseline to reopen the Clear Baseline dialog box

6 Select Clear interim plan, select Start 1/Finish 1, select Selected tasks and click OK

Backward-Scheduling

The default method of scheduling is forward-scheduling from the project start date. This is what we have been using in all the examples so far. However, there may be times when you have to complete a project by a certain date. By scheduling backwards from a finish date, you can see when a project has to start. However, there is a right and a wrong way to go about this.

The Right Way

Use backward-scheduling right from the start. When you first create your project, set it to schedule back from the required completion date before you input any tasks:

1 Create a new project and select Project Information from the Project ribbon. Select Schedule from: Project Finish Date, enter the required finish date for the project and click OK

Then, as you input your tasks and allocate resources, Project will correctly backward-schedule your project. But what if you start off with forward-scheduling and then decide you need to switch to backward-scheduling?

The Wrong Way

Project will allow you to change from forward-scheduling to backward-scheduling, but it doesn't always work out too well. So make sure you save your project file before trying this.

1 Open your project in Gantt Chart view, select Show Outline Level 1 and select Entire Project from the View ribbon, to get the whole project into view

2 Select Project Information from the Project ribbon, change Schedule from: to Project Finish Date, enter the required finish date and click OK

3 Accept any warnings and carry on until the project has been rescheduled

Sometimes this works and sometimes it doesn't. If it worked, save the project with a new name. If it didn't work, you may have to start again by creating a new project (the right way).

Beware

Scheduling back from a finish date is more difficult and should be avoided until you have some experience of forward-scheduling.

Summary

- User controlled scheduling allows you to schedule tasks manually and leave part of the scheduling information blank, or with text placeholders for later completion

- Automatic scheduling involves Project taking the tasks, the resources allocated to them, and the resource calendars to work out the best time for each task to start and finish

- Work is the effort that will be required to complete a task (usually expressed in hours), duration is the length of time it will actually take (usually measured in days), and units are the resources that will be used to complete a task (expressed as a percentage, where 100% = one full resource)

- Fixed unit tasks are the default, where the units (resource percentage) remain constant and duration or work effort changes according to the number of resources allocated

- Fixed duration tasks with effort-driven scheduling will split the work between the resources, if more resources are added. With non-effort-driven scheduling, it will increase the work if more resources are added

- Fixed work tasks will only adjust duration and resource units, so adding a resource will reduce the resource percentage

- After a change, you can over-ride the way Project has rescheduled by using the smart tag in the task information box

- Resource contouring is the process of applying a different availability (unit percentage) over a series of time periods

- Contouring is the process of ramping work on a task up and down, and there are seven contour profiles that can be applied in addition to flat (the default)

- Baselines and interim plans represent snapshots of the project schedule at set points in time. They can be set, cleared and updated (replaced)

- Backward-scheduling is an option in Project but, if it is to be used, it should be used from the start of the project, if at all possible

11 Conflicts and Constraints

This chapter deals with resource conflicts and using leveling to resolve them. It also introduces task constraints, project calculation and moving a project.

Resource Conflicts

As you begin to assign resources to tasks and then make subsequent changes to tasks and schedules, you may begin to get resource conflicts. A resource conflict is where a resource is scheduled to perform more work than it can carry out in the time available. Project flags these conflicts for you by highlighting the relevant resource information in red and flagging the tasks causing the overallocation. Project provides a number of tools and options for dealing with these:

1 In Gantt Chart view, position your cursor over a flag

		Task Name	Duration	Start	Jul 15, '13	Jul 22, '13
					14 15 16 17 18 19 20 21	22 23 24 25 26 27
5		1.4 Identify Business Case	2 days	07/16/13	Prudence Project	
6		1.5 Risk Analysis	1 day	07/16/13	Prudence Project	
7		This task has overallocated resources. Right-click for options.	1 day	07/18/13	Prudence Project	
8		1.7 Project Approval	5 days	07/19/13		07/25

2 Right-click on the task to bring up the options (as illustrated right)

3 Select Reschedule to Available Date to move to the first available date for this resource and remove the overallocation

4 Select Ignore Problems for This Task to keep the overallocation but remove the flag

5 Select Inactivate Task, Manually Schedule, Auto Schedule or Assign Resources to perform these actions

6 Select Fix in Task Inspector to open Task Inspector (as illustrated right)

Task Inspector displays some similar options (the Ignore option being to de-select the tick at the bottom) together with further information on the task, predecessor tasks, resource and reason for the overallocation.

Beware

The options list on the right has been abbreviated. There are several more options but they are not relevant to this topic.

Don't forget

The Team Planner option in Task Inspector is not available in Project Standard.

Fix in Task Inspector...
Reschedule to Available Date
Ignore Problems for This Task
Insert Task
Delete Task
Inactivate Task
Manually Schedule
Auto Schedule
Assign Resources...
Fill Down
Clear Contents
Information...
Notes...

Task Inspector ✕

⚠ 6 - Risk Analysis

Resources overallocated due to work on other tasks
Prudence Project

ACTIONS:
➔■ Move task to resources' next available time.
Reschedule Task

📋 View overallocated resources in Team Planner.
Team Planner

INFO:
Auto Scheduled
Start: 07/16/13
Finish: 07/16/13

Predecessor Tasks:

Name	Type	Lag
5 - Identify Business Case	Start To Start	0 days

☑ Show warning and suggestion indicators for this task.

In Resource Usage and other resource views, overallocated resources will be highlighted in red, as will the days on which overallocation occurs. Use Next Overallocation on the Resource ribbon to bring the overallocation into view (as illustrated below).

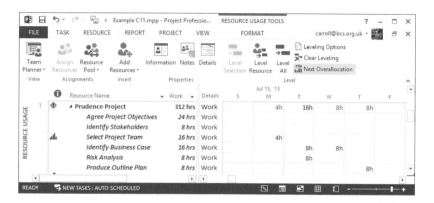

In the example above, the resource name on the summary line is highlighted in red, together with the Tuesday where we have created an overallocation of 16 hours. The details of the tasks are shown below the summary line, so that you can see exactly which tasks have caused the problem. The work can be adjusted in Team Planner (see page 88), if you have Project Professional, otherwise, Resource Allocation view provides some useful data.

Team Planner is not available in Project Standard.

7 Select View > More Views > Resource Allocation from the Resource ribbon and click the Apply button:

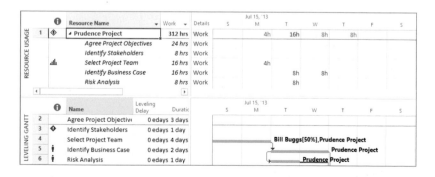

Each overallocated task can be examined and the appropriate option selected for dealing with it (covered in the next two topics). Use Next Overallocation to move on to the next task.

131

Resource Leveling

In Project, resource conflicts can be resolved either manually or automatically. The process used to resolve these conflicts is called resource leveling.

1 Select View > More Views > Resource Allocation from the Resource ribbon and click the Apply button

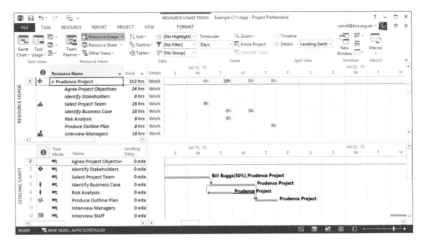

2 Select Project Information from the Project ribbon and note the current project finish date

3 Select the lower (Leveling Gantt) panel so that it is active

4 Select Level Resource from the Resource ribbon to open the Level Resource dialog box (as illustrated right)

5 Select the resource (or resources by holding down the Ctrl key) that you wish to level and click the Level Now button

If you receive any warnings that Project cannot resolve some over-allocations, make a note of the dates and click on the Skip button to continue. You will need to deal with these by using manual adjustments (covered in the next topic).

Resource Leveling Issue

There are some issues with Project when carrying out resource leveling. In the example, we allocated our project manager to a task (2.1.1 Interview Managers) at 100%, so the 2 days work was scheduled as 2 days duration.

We then reduced the project manager's availability to 50% for September (on page 121), but it did not change the schedule (causing an overallocation). Now we have performed resource leveling, but Project cannot cope with this. It has scheduled the first day on July 29 (100% available) but then split the task and scheduled the second day on September 02 (when the resource is available 100% again). This is clearly not right, but we can fix it.

		Task Name	Duration	Start	
10		⊿ 2.1 Interviews	29 days	07/24/13	
11		2.1.1 Interview Managers	2 days	07/29/13	Prudence Project,Travel[$200.00]
12		2.1.2 Interview Staff	2 days	07/24/13	Prudence Project
13		2.2 Draft Requirements	2 days	09/03/13	Prudence Project
14		2.3 Feedback Sessions	1 day	09/05/13	Prudence Project,Bill Buggs

1   Select the task and click on Assign Resources on the Resource ribbon to open the Assign Resources dialog box

2   Select the resource and click the Remove button, then select the same resource and click the Assign button (the task is rescheduled for two days and flagged for the overallocation)

3   Now select Details from the View ribbon and change the task to Fixed Work (see page 120). Increase the duration to 3 days (the first day at 100% and the next two at 50%, in line with the resource availability) and the overallocation flag is removed, as illustrated below

		Task Name	Duration	Start	
10		⊿ 2.1 Interviews	6 days	07/24/13	
11		2.1.1 Interview Managers	3 days	07/29/13	Prudence Project,Travel[$200.00]
12		2.1.2 Interview Staff	2 days	07/24/13	Prudence Project
13		2.2 Draft Requirements	2 days	08/01/13	Prudence Project
14		2.3 Feedback Sessions	1 day	08/05/13	Prudence Project,E
15		2.4 Finalize Requirements	2 days	08/06/13	Prudence F

Beware

This is a known issue and can be avoided if tasks are only allocated at a single rate of availability.

Manual Adjustments

In addition to using resource leveling to automatically resolve resource conflicts, you will also need to resolve some conflicts manually. This may be necessary if you do not want Project to extend the schedule, or (as in the previous topic) where Project cannot resolve the conflict.

Resolving a conflict manually can involve a number of options:

- Allocating more resources to a task

- Rescheduling or splitting a task

- Reallocating tasks to a different resource

- Adding overtime working

We will look at each of these in turn.

Allocating More Resources

To add additional resources to a task, select the task and click on Assign Resources from the Resource ribbon (see Fixed Unit Tasks on page 118 for an example).

Rescheduling a Task

The easiest way to reschedule a task that is causing an overallocation is to change the start date or drag it to another time, when the resource is available (see Moving Linked Tasks on page 79 for an example). When moving a linked task, you may receive Planning Wizard warnings (also covered on page 79) which necessitate removing links. So, following this rescheduling, you should re-link the moved task in an appropriate way.

In a similar way, we can split a task and move the split parts to times when the required resource is available (see Splitting Tasks on page 78).

Reallocating Tasks

Select the task, click Assign Resources on the Resource ribbon to open the Assign Resources dialog box (as illustrated), click the Replace button and select the new resource from the list when prompted.

Don't forget

You can also reallocate tasks in Team Planner view if you have Project Professional.

Overtime Working

In addition to allocating more resources, rescheduling or reallocating a task, we can leave a task allocated where it is but complete it sooner by scheduling overtime working.

In the following example, let us say that we need to have task 4.1 (Design Work) completed as early as possible, and the resource assigned to it has agreed to work two additional hours (overtime) per day on this task.

1   Note the days that the task is being carried out

2   Select Change Working Time from the Project ribbon and select the appropriate resource calendar

3   Enter a description on the Exception tab and the Start and Finish dates

4   Click the Details button and enter the working time to include the two additional agreed hours per day

Beware

As these working days span a weekend, the fourth day needs to be made a separate exception.

The duration of the task remains 5 days but the work is now completed in 4 days, due to the 2 additional hours being worked per day by the allocated resource. In this example it has also resulted in the task becoming non-critical.

Task Constraints

When tasks are first entered into a project, they have the project start date as their start date (unless the project is backwards-scheduled, in which case, they have the project finish date as their finish date). As they are linked and have resources assigned to them, they will be scheduled depending on their dependencies and resource availability and be given their own start and finish dates.

Sometimes these allocated start and finish dates are not viable in the real world and a start or finish date has to be imposed. When this happens in Project, it is called setting a task constraint.

Task constraints are set in the form of: must start or finish on a particular date; start no earlier or later than a particular date; finish no earlier or later than a particular date; start as soon as possible; or finish as late as possible. The default constraint which is applied to all tasks on a forward-scheduled project is: start as soon as possible. For a backward-scheduled project, the default constraint is start as late as possible.

Constraints can also be flexible or inflexible. A flexible constraint is one where the project finish date can be moved by the task. An inflexible constraint is one where the project finish date cannot be moved by the task. The following table lists the flexible constraint types and any limitations on that flexibility:

Constraint	Flexible for
As Soon As Possible	All projects
As Late As Possible	All projects
Finish No Earlier Than	Forward-scheduled projects
Start No Earlier Than	Forward-scheduled projects
Finish No Later Than	Backward-scheduled projects
Start No Later Than	Backward-scheduled projects

The "As Soon As Possible" and "As Late As Possible" constraints do not use a date, while all the others have a date associated with them. The date is the earliest or latest date that the task can or must start or finish (as appropriate to the type of constraint).

Applying Constraints

The usual reason for applying a constraint to a task is that some internal or external factor means that it can only happen at a certain time. As an example, a good time to start using a new financial system is often the start of a new financial year. So, in this case, you might want to set a "start no earlier" constraint.

1 In Gantt Chart view, select the task you wish to apply the constraint to and double-click on the Task Name to open the Task Information dialog box

	ⓘ	Task Name	Duration	Start	Oct 14, '13 14 15 16 17 18 19 20	Oct 21, '13 21 22 23 24 25 26
31		⁴ 5 Implementation Stage	40 days	10/15/13		
32		5.1 Train Users	5 days	10/15/13		
33		5.2 Convert to New System	5 days	10/22/13		
34		5.3 Parallel Run	20 days	10/29/13		
35		5.4 Contingency	10 days	11/26/13		

2 Select the General tab and note the task's current start and finish dates

3 Then select the Advanced tab, select the constraint type, set the constraint date, click OK and accept any warnings

In this example, we have set a constraint of Start No Earlier than January 01. The constraint is set, the schedule is adjusted and a constraint symbol is added to the task information box.

	ⓘ	Task Name	Duration	Start	'13 07	Nov '13 14 21 28 04 11 18 25	Dec '13 02 09 16 23	Jan '14 30 06 13 20 27	Feb '14 03 10 17
31		⁴ 5 Implementation Stage	89 days	10/15/13					
32		5.1 Train Users	5 days	10/15/13					
33		5.2 Convert to New System	5 days	01/01/14					
34		This task has a 'Start No Earlier Than' constraint on 01/01/14.	20 days	01/08/14					
35		5.4 Contingency	10 days	02/05/14					

As usual, you can view the details of the constraint by positioning your pointer over the constraint symbol (as illustrated above).

Note: this has effectively introduced a two and a half month lag time between this task and the preceding task, in consequence the earlier tasks are no longer on the critical path.

Hot tip

In practice, you would also want training to start as close as possible to the conversion date (a start "as late as possible" constraint would achieve this).

Constraint Conflicts

If you set a constraint that causes a conflict, the Planning Wizard appears to warn you of the problem and to offer suggestions for how you may be able to deal with it. As an example, we will force a constraint conflict by setting a "must finish on" constraint on task 2.7.2 Present to Management (below).

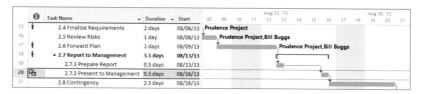

1 Double-click on the relevant task to open the Task Information dialog box and check the current dates in the General tab

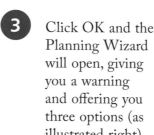

2 On the Advanced tab, we will set a Must Finish On constraint, with the date of the preceding Friday

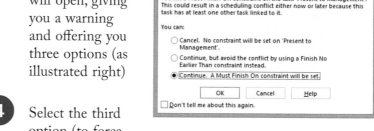

3 Click OK and the Planning Wizard will open, giving you a warning and offering you three options (as illustrated right)

4 Select the third option (to force the constraint), click OK, accept any further warning and the task will be rescheduled

In the example above, the task has been scheduled before two tasks it is dependant on are completed. You would not normally want to introduce this type of constraint conflict, so, in practice, you should select Cancel at step 4 and find another alternative.

Viewing Constraints

When a task has a constraint applied to it, there will be a constraint symbol in the task's information box. The constraint symbol looks like a small calendar, and it will have a blue dot if it is a flexible constraint and a red dot if it is an inflexible constraint. If you pause your pointer over it, a pop-up will display details of the constraint.

1 In Gantt Chart view, pause your pointer over a constraint symbol (the example on the right is the constraint set on the previous page)

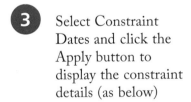

You can also view constraints by applying the Constraints Dates table to the Gantt Chart view.

2 Select Table > More Tables from the View ribbon to display the More Tables dialog box (illustrated right)

3 Select Constraint Dates and click the Apply button to display the constraint details (as below)

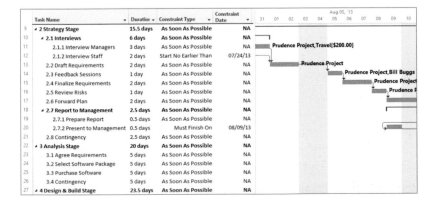

Calculate Project

By default, Project re-calculates the project schedule each time you make a change. You can suppress this and decide when you want Project to re-calculate and re-schedule the project.

1 Select Options from the File ribbon to open the Project Options dialog box

2 Select Schedule from the options list on the left hand side (as illustrated below)

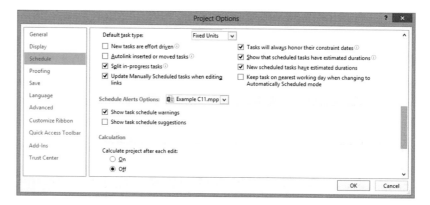

3 Use the scroll bar on the right hand side to scroll down until you reach the Calculation section (as illustrated above)

4 Select the Off option to turn automatic calculation off and click OK

5 Once you have completed the changes to your project, select Calculate Project from the Project ribbon (as illustrated below) and the project will be re-scheduled

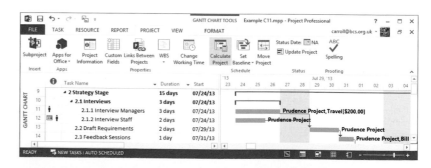

Move Project

Changing the project start will not automatically and correctly re-schedule every task in the project. This is due to the task dependencies and any constraints that have been applied. Move Project gets around this problem. It is also very handy if you want to use an old project as a template for a new one.

1 Open the old project, or the project that is to be moved, in Gantt Chart view (this example is from Project 2007):

2 Select Move Project from the Project ribbon (as illustrated above) and the Move Project dialog box opens

3 Select the New start date, select Move deadlines (if the deadlines are to move in step) and click OK

The project is rescheduled and dependencies and constraints are honored wherever possible. But it is worth scrolling through the whole project to check that no anomalies have crept in (as in the illustration below, where some tasks have not been rescheduled).

		Task Name	Duration	Start	
1		▲ 1 Initiation Stage	13 days	07/03/07	
2		1.1 Agree Project Objectives	1 day	08/01/13	Prudence Project
3	◆	1.2 Identify Stakeholders	1 day	08/02/13	Prudence Project
4		1.3 Identify Project Team	2 days	08/05/13	Bill Buggs,Prudence Project
5		1.4 Identify Business Case	1 day	07/09/07	
6		1.5 Analyse the Risks	1 day	07/11/07	
7	✎	1.6 Produce Outline Project Plan	1 day	08/12/13	Prudence Project
8		1.7 Project Approval	0 days	08/19/07	
9		▲ 2 Strategy Stage	15.5 days	07/20/07	
10		▲ 2.1 Carry out Interviews	2 days	07/20/07	
11		2.1.1 Interview Managers	2 days	08/19/13	
12	▦	2.1.2 Interview Staff	2 days	08/19/13	

Summary

- Resource conflicts occur when the scheduled work cannot be carried out by the assigned resources in the required time frame

- Task Inspector provides useful help and guidance for dealing with these conflicts and there is a drop down menu available by right-clicking a task

- Project offers two options for resource leveling: manual (where you tell it when to level) and automatic (where leveling is performed continually)

- Project may have difficulty with leveling if you have used resource profiling (varying percentage availability)

- Manual adjustments can be made by allocating more resources to a task, rescheduling or splitting a task, reallocating tasks to a different resource, or overtime working

- Task constraints can be applied manually or through the leveling process and they determine when a task can or must start or finish

- Constraints can be applied on the advanced tab of the Task Information dialog box, or by setting the start or end date of a task

- Project will flag a constraint conflict if a constraint you are trying to apply can or will have an impact on another task

- Tasks with a constraint will have a constraint symbol in their task information box or details of all constraints can be displayed by applying the constraints dates table

- By default, Project re-calculates and re-schedules every time you make a change to a project, but this can be turned off in Project Options and the project will only be scheduled when you select Calculate Project from the Project ribbon

- Move Project allows you to change the project start data and re-schedule the whole project. It is also useful if you want to use an old project as a template for a new one. However, anomalies can creep in and it is still important to check the whole project

12 Viewing Data

Project holds a vast amount of information on your project and provides many options for selecting and viewing it. This chapter covers the different ways of viewing, grouping, filtering, sorting and displaying the information.

Views

In Project, views are the way that data is displayed for you to look at and work on. They can be placed into two main categories: task views and resource views. There are 20 task views and 7 resource views. You normally use task views when working with task information and resource views when working with resource information. The views can be further divided into sheets, charts, graphs and forms.

Sheets

Sheets (similar to spreadsheets) display information in rows and columns, with each task or resource being a row (horizontal) and each field in the task or resource being a column (vertical).

Charts and Graphs

Charts display graphical information in chart form, typical examples being the Gantt Chart and Network Diagram views. Graphs are used to display statistical information graphically in views, such as Resource Graph and Calendar.

Forms

Forms are used for the display and entry of detailed information on a task or resource.

Some views (such as Calendar) are simple, single views and some are compound views (such as Gantt Chart, which shows a sheet on the left and a chart on the right). You can also display a single view or two views (one above the other). The example below is a compound view with the Gantt Chart (table and chart) in the upper half and the Task Form in the lower half.

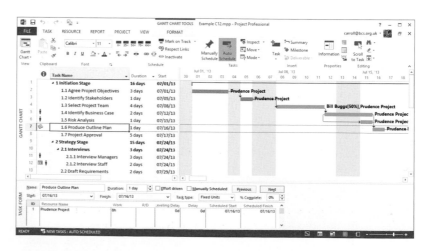

Tables

When working in a sheet view, there are a number of preset tables that can be used (applied) to access different types of information on tasks or resources. There are 17 task tables that can be applied to task views and 10 resource tables applicable to resource views.

If the view you have currently selected is not displaying quite the right information, you can apply a different table to change the view. The tasks or resources displayed remain the same but you will see different bits of information for them.

1 In Gantt Chart view, select Task Usage from the View ribbon to replace the Task Entry view

	Task Name	Duration	Start	Details	M	T	W	T	F	S	S	M	T
					Jul 01, '13							Jul 08, '13	
1	◢ Initiation Stage	16 days	07/01/13	Work	8h	8h	8h		8h			5.2h	7.6h
2	◢ Agree Project Objectives	3 days	07/01/13	Work	8h	8h	8h						
	Prudence Project		07/01/13	Work	8h	8h	8h						
3	◢ Identify Stakeholders	1 day	07/05/13	Work					8h				
	Prudence Project		07/05/13	Work					8h				
4	◢ Select Project Team	4 days	07/08/13	Work								5.2h	7.6h
	Prudence Project		07/08/13	Work								1.2h	3.6h
	Bill Buggs		07/08/13	Work								4h	4h
5	◢ Identify Business Case	2 days	07/12/13	Work									
	Prudence Project		07/12/13	Work									
6	◢ Risk Analysis	1 day	07/15/13	Work									
	Prudence Project		07/15/13	Work									

2 Then select Tables from the View ribbon and select Work from the built-in drop down list to show the work details

	Task Name	Work	Baseline	Variance	Actual	Remaining	Details	T	W	T	F	S
1	◢ Initiation Stage	88 hrs	88 hrs	0 hrs	0 hrs	88 hrs	Work	8h	8h		8h	
2	◢ Agree Project Objectives	24 hrs	24 hrs	0 hrs	0 hrs	24 hrs	Work	8h	8h			
	Prudence Project	24 hrs	24 hrs	0 hrs	0 hrs	24 hrs	Work	8h	8h			
3	◢ Identify Stakeholders	8 hrs	8 hrs	0 hrs	0 hrs	8 hrs	Work				8h	
	Prudence Project	8 hrs	8 hrs	0 hrs	0 hrs	8 hrs	Work				8h	
4	◢ Select Project Team	24 hrs	24 hrs	0 hrs	0 hrs	24 hrs	Work					
	Prudence Project	16 hrs	16 hrs	0 hrs	0 hrs	16 hrs	Work					
	Bill Buggs	8 hrs	8 hrs	0 hrs	0 hrs	8 hrs	Work					
5	◢ Identify Business Case	16 hrs	16 hrs	0 hrs	0 hrs	16 hrs	Work					
	Prudence Project	16 hrs	16 hrs	0 hrs	0 hrs	16 hrs	Work					
6	◢ Risk Analysis	8 hrs	8 hrs	0 hrs	0 hrs	8 hrs	Work					
	Prudence Project	8 hrs	8 hrs	0 hrs	0 hrs	8 hrs	Work					
7	◢ Produce Outline Plan	8 hrs	8 hrs	0 hrs	0 hrs	8 hrs	Work					
	Prudence Project	8 hrs	8 hrs	0 hrs	0 hrs	8 hrs	Work					
8	Project Approval	0 hrs	0 hrs	0 hrs	0 hrs	0 hrs	Work					
9	◢ Strategy Stage	132 hrs	140 hrs	-8 hrs	0 hrs	132 hrs	Work					
10	◢ Interviews	32 hrs	32 hrs	0 hrs	0 hrs	32 hrs	Work					
11	◢ Interview Managers	16 hrs	16 hrs	0 hrs	0 hrs	16 hrs	Work					
	Prudence Project	16 hrs	0 hrs	16 hrs	0 hrs	16 hrs	Work					

3 Try applying the various different tables to the views that you use to see what is available

4 When you have finished, you can apply the default view back by selecting Gantt Chart from the View ribbon (the Table will automatically switch back to Entry)

Grouping

Grouping allows you to view your project tasks or resources grouped by any defined criteria. This can be applied to most, but not all, task and resource views. Each view has various standard groups to select from.

1 In Resource Sheet view, click the down arrow next to Group By on the View ribbon to get the drop-down list

2 Select Resource Group in the drop-down list and the resource sheet is rearranged by resource within group, as in the following illustration

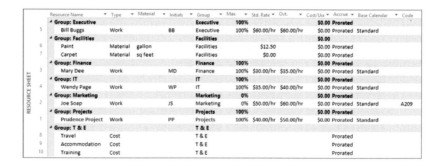

3 Try selecting the various other Group By options in the drop-down list

4 To return to the standard view, just select No Groups in the Group By options

5 In Gantt Chart view, click the down arrow next to Group By on the View ribbon to get the drop-down list and select Constraint Type (see the following example)

...cont'd

Following Step 5 opposite, the tasks are now grouped under the constraint types, as illustrated below.

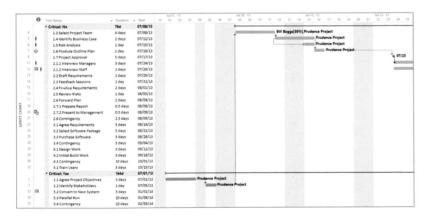

This is a useful view to see which constraints you have set on which tasks. The Summary Tasks group behaves in the same way as the normal summary tasks, and the view can be expanded and contracted by clicking on the small triangle sign in front of the group name.

The other useful feature is that Project rolls up totals by these groupings for you, useful for monitoring costs and work effort.

6 In Gantt Chart view, select Group By > Critical from the View ribbon to apply this new grouping to the Gantt Chart view

7 Next select Tables from the View ribbon and Work from the drop down list to display the rolled-up work effort totals on the critical and non-critical summary lines

8 Now try out the other Group By options on the Gantt Chart view and also take a look at the group by options on the other views

Hot tip

Note: the constraint type As Soon As Possible has been closed up in this illustration, as most tasks are in this default group.

Hot tip

In addition to the 12 predefined task and 6 predefined resource groupings, you can also create your own new groupings.

Fiscal Year

Project provides a fiscal year option for use in the timescale above Gantt and other charts. The following example shows how this can be used when the fiscal (business) year is different from the calendar year.

1 Select Options from the File menu and then select the Schedule option on the left hand side (as below)

2 Change "Fiscal year starts in:" to April, select "Use starting year for FY numbering" and click OK to close the Project Options dialog box

3 Select the down arrow beneath Timescale on the View ribbon and select Timescale from the bottom of the drop down list to open the Timescale dialog box

4 On the Middle Tier, set Units to Years and deselect "Use fiscal year".
On the Bottom Tier set Units to Quarters, select "Use fiscal year" and

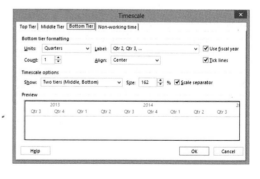

click OK. The major timescale now displays calendar years and the minor scale displays fiscal quarters (as below)

Filters

In addition to its other selection capabilities, Project also allows you to filter and sort data before viewing (or printing). Filtering allows you to select just the information you wish to be displayed.

Predefined Filters

There are a number of predefined filters you can use to select things, such as late tasks, tasks in progress, work that is over budget, and so on. Project contains 45 predefined task and 25 predefined resource filters. In addition to these, you can also create your own custom filters to meet any specific requirements.

Filters can be used to focus on certain tasks in your project or on specific resources in the project. When you apply a filter, only the tasks or resources that meet the filter criteria are displayed. All other tasks and resources are hidden while you are using a filter.

Applying filters to your project does not change the data in any way, it just changes the way it is displayed.

AutoFilter

Project contains an AutoFilter feature that gives you a quick way of finding particular information in a field. When it's turned on (the default setting), each column heading has an arrow on the right-hand side that can be used to apply a filter to the information in that column. You can apply filters to as many columns as you like and, once a filter has been applied to a column, a filter symbol will appear next to the column title (see illustration on page 150).

Interactive Filters

As well as specific filters, you can apply interactive filters that display a dialog box during the filtering process. You then provide the information to the dialog box to allow Project to complete the filtering process.

Custom Filters

If none of the predefined filters meet your requirements, you can define a new custom filter that exactly matches your needs. You can copy an existing filter and then edit it to meet your needs or you can create a completely new filter. The Filter Definition dialog box provides shortcuts to simplify this process.

Examples of these filters types are given over the next few topics.

AutoFilter

When AutoFilter is turned on (down arrow in each column), you can apply filters to any column. Select All and Clear All Filters options will remove any filter criteria, and the Filters > Custom option allows a column to be filtered by more than one criterion. The following example will demonstrate filtering on task duration.

Hot tip

AutoFilter can be set on or off for all new projects from File Menu Options > Advanced.

1 In Gantt Chart view, if AutoFilter is not already on select Filter from the View ribbon and select Display Auto Filter from the drop down list to display the filter down arrows in each column header

2 Select Tables from the View ribbon and select Usage from the drop down list to apply the Usage table

3 Click the Duration down arrow, select Filters, Greater than and then "is greater than" and "1 day" in the Custom Auto Filter dialog box (right) and note the filter symbol in the Duration column heading, indicating a filter has been applied to the data, as illustrated below

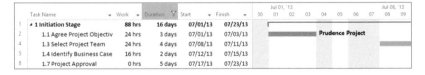

Hot tip

You can save any AutoFilter setting as a Custom filter for future use by clicking the Save button on the left.

4 Click the Duration down arrow, select Filters > Custom

5 Select the required filters from the drop down lists or enter the required values and click OK

6 Click the Duration down arrow and Clear Filters from Duration to turn the filter off again

Filter Criteria

You can specify filter criteria interactively if you often need to make similar enquiries but with slightly different parameters. This is preferable to creating a large number of custom filters.

For example, you might want to get details of all tasks that are scheduled during the summer, to check for any vacation implications.

1 Select Other Views > More Views > Task Sheet from the View ribbon, click Apply, then select Tables > Schedule

2 Select Filter > Date Range from the View ribbon to open the first (From) Date Range dialog box

3 Enter or select the From date (as on the right) and click OK

4 Enter or select the To date and click OK to display only the tasks in the selected range

	Task Name	Start	Finish	Late	Late
9	▲ **Strategy Stage**	**07/24/13**	**08/13/13**	**10/02/13**	**10/25/13**
15	Finalize Requirements	08/01/13	08/02/13	10/10/13	10/14/13
16	Review Risks	08/05/13	08/05/13	10/14/13	10/15/13
17	Forward Plan	08/06/13	08/07/13	10/15/13	10/17/13
18	▲ **Report to Management**	**08/08/13**	**08/09/13**	**10/17/13**	**10/18/13**
19	Prepare Report	08/08/13	08/08/13	10/17/13	10/17/13
20	Present to Management	08/09/13	08/09/13	10/18/13	10/18/13
21	Contingency	08/09/13	08/13/13	10/23/13	10/25/13
22	▲ **Analysis Stage**	**08/14/13**	**09/10/13**	**10/28/13**	**11/22/13**
23	Agree Requirements	08/14/13	08/20/13	10/28/13	11/01/13
24	Select Software Package	08/21/13	08/27/13	11/04/13	11/08/13
25	Purchase Software	08/28/13	09/03/13	11/11/13	11/15/13

Hot tip

The two Late columns are the latest start and finish dates that will still keep the project on the critical path.

5 Select the Filter down arrow on the View ribbon and select No Filter from the drop down list to remove any filters that have been applied

Filter by Resource

You can use resource filters in a Task view to display all tasks assigned to a resource. In a Resource view, you can use resource filters to select resources by Group.

1 In Gantt Chart view, click the Filter down arrow on the View ribbon and select Using Resource... (the three dots indicate further choices)

2 Click the down arrow, select the resource name (as illustrated) and click OK

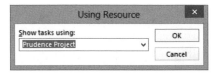

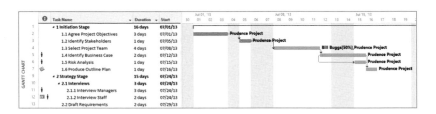

Note that, in the above example, all tasks assigned to the selected resource will be displayed (including tasks with additional resources assigned). The next example will filter by resource group in a resource view.

3 In Resource Sheet view, click the Filter down arrow on the View ribbon and select Group...

4 Type in the name of the group and click OK to filter by the resource group

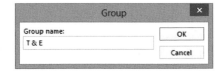

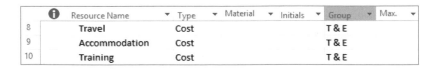

5 To remove Resource or Group filters, click the Filter down arrow on the View ribbon and select (No Filter) from the drop down list

Beware

There is no selection facility in the Group dialog box, you have to type the group name.

Sorting

Tasks and Resources are usually displayed in ascending ID Number sequence. However, you can sort the display by any field or a combination of fields by specifying sort keys.

The following example will identify the largest pieces of work by sorting the tasks by summary task and then tasks in descending duration sequence.

1 In Task Sheet view, select Outline > All Subtasks from the View ribbon and then select Tables > Usage

2 Select Sort > Sort By from View ribbon to open the Sort dialog box, as illustrated below

3 Click on the Sort by down arrow, select Summary and select Descending, as illustrated right

4 Click on the Then by down arrow, select Duration and Descending, as illustrated above

5 Uncheck Keep outline structure (bottom of the Sort dialog box) and click the Sort button to sort the tasks into the desired sequence, as illustrated below

	ⓘ	Task Name	Work	Duration	Start	Finish
1		▲ 1 Initiation Stage	88 hrs	16 days	07/01/13	07/23/13
9		▲ 2 Strategy Stage	132 hrs	15 days	07/24/13	08/13/13
10		▲ 2.1 Interviews	32 hrs	3 days	07/24/13	07/26/13
18		▲ 2.7 Report to Management	12 hrs	1.5 days	08/08/13	08/09/13
34		5.3 Parallel Run	0 hrs	20 days	01/08/14	02/04/14
30		4.3 Contingency	0 hrs	10 days	10/01/13	10/14/13
35		5.4 Contingency	0 hrs	10 days	02/05/14	02/18/14
8		1.7 Project Approval	0 hrs	5 days	07/17/13	07/23/13
23		3.1 Agree Requirements	40 hrs	5 days	08/14/13	08/20/13
24		3.2 Select Software Package	40 hrs	5 days	08/21/13	08/27/13
25		3.3 Purchase Software	40 hrs	5 days	08/28/13	09/03/13
26		3.4 Contingency	0 hrs	5 days	09/04/13	09/10/13
28		4.1 Design Work	40 hrs	5 days	09/11/13	09/17/13

Hot tip

Combining sorting with filters gives you a powerful range of features for viewing your data.

Highlight Filters

When Tasks and Resources are filtered, those that do not meet the filter criteria are hidden from view. Highlight filters can be used so that all tasks or resources remain visible, but the tasks or resources that meet the filter criteria are highlighted.

1 In Gantt Chart view, select Outline > All subtasks from the View ribbon and select Highlight > More Filters from the View ribbon to open the More Filters dialog box

2 Select the required filter criteria (Resource Group in this example) and click the Highlight button

3 The Resource Group dialog box will open, type in the name of the resource group to be filtered (Executive in this example) and click OK

The resources belonging to the selected resource group will be highlighted, as in the following example.

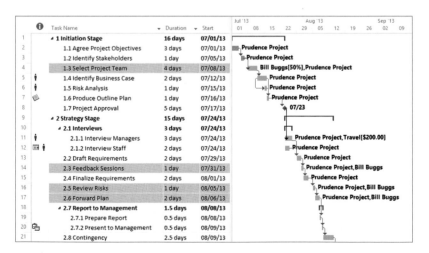

4 Click the Highlight down arrow on the View ribbon and select No Highlight from the drop down list to return the display to normal again

Fonts and Highlighting

The Font group of functions allows you to change the font characteristics of text (font, style, size and text color) and also the background color and pattern of cells or rows, to convey additional meaning to the data. For example, we may wish to highlight certain problem tasks in a report to management.

1 In Gantt Chart view, select the task you wish to highlight by clicking on the Task ID (to select the whole task) and select the link in the bottom right of the Font group on the Task ribbon to open the Font dialog box

2 Select the down arrow beside Background Color: and select the desired color from the drop-down list

3 Select Background Pattern and click OK

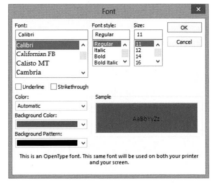

155

You can also use the font color, background and other functions direct in the Font group.

As well as applying background highlighting, the Font dialog box allows you to edit the font characteristics. There are also individual functions in the Font group for most characteristics, such as bold and size. This gives significant scope for highlighting.

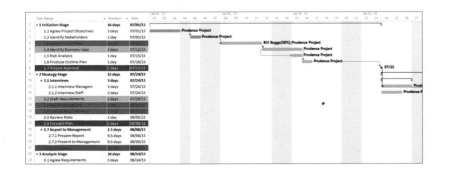

If you select a dark background color, it will improve readability if you change the font to a light color.

Custom Fields

Project allows you to define, store and manipulate custom data, set up lists of acceptable values to make data entry more accurate, set formulae to perform calculations on the data and use graphic indicators to represent data. In the following example, we will set up a custom field to contain task risks.

1 In Gantt Chart view, select Custom Fields from the Project ribbon

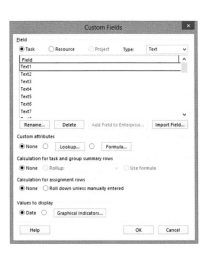

2 Select Text for the Type (as illustrated) and click the Rename button

3 In the Rename Field dialog box type in the name (Risk)

4 Now click Lookup, enter the values (High, Medium, Low and None), select a default (None), click Close and click OK

5 Right-click on the heading of the Start column and select Insert Column

To lookup a field in a long list start typing the name you are looking for and the list will scroll down to the name.

6 Scroll down to find the new field Text1 (Risk) and select it

7 Now type in or select the risk for each task (any new tasks created will be allocated the default None)

Graphic Indicators

In the previous topic, we set up a Custom field for risk and inserted a new column into the Gantt chart Entry table for it. We can now allocate a graphic indicator (traffic signal) to the risk field for visual impact.

1 In Gantt Chart view, right-click on the column heading of the relevant field (Risk) and select Custom Fields to open the Custom Fields dialog box (as illustrated opposite top)

2 Click the Graphic Indicators button to open the Graphic Indicators dialog box, as below

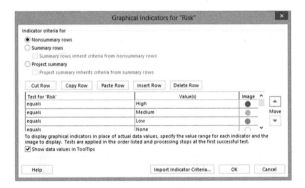

3 Using the drop-down arrows, select Test for Risk "equals", Value "High" and Image "red stop light" as above

4 Repeat for the other three values (Medium, Low and None), using appropriate yellow, green and white images

5 Click OK twice and your risks will now be graphic

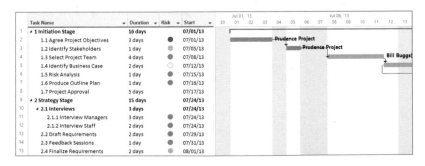

Summary

- Views are the ways that Project displays data on the screen; they consist of sheets (like spreadsheets), charts and graphs (visual) and forms (for detailed data entry)

- When working in a sheet view, there are a number of different tables that can be applied to vary the data in the sheet

- Grouping allows you to group the data by resource and various other options

- Fiscal year allows you to work with a non-calendar year

- Filters enable you to select which tasks or resources are displayed, according to selection criteria

- AutoFilter enables you to select a filter on one or more columns

- Filter criteria allow you to specify more complex filters based on ranges or comparisons

- Tasks and resources can be filtered by resource or resource group

- In addition to filtering, sorting allows the sequence in which tasks or other data are displayed to be defined, using up to three parameters

- Highlight filters allow all data to remain visible but with the data that meets the filter criteria being highlighted in yellow

- Background cell highlighting allows cells or rows to be highlighted in various colors independent of the data, for information purposes

- In addition to the background highlighting, the fonts can also be varied, as required

- Custom Fields allow you to define, store and manipulate custom data, set up lists of values to validate data entry and perform calculations on your data

- You can add custom fields into existing tables or create new tables containing them

- Graphic Indicators allow you to select appropriate images (such as traffic signals) to replace data values

⑬ Reports

This chapter covers the setup, preview and printing of charts and reports. It deals with visual reports, the useful copy picture and report functions and some of the other new features introduced in Project 2013.

Printing a View

Any chart or table view can be printed using the print function on the File ribbon. However, it is worthwhile setting the view up correctly before you print it.

1 For example, to print a Gantt Chart view, first format the screen to show the information you want to appear on the print by showing the appropriate level of subtasks and zooming in or out as required

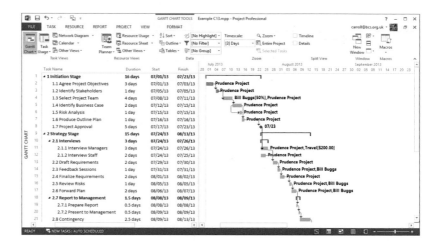

2 Then move the middle vertical divider to cover or expose required fields on the table (left-hand panel)

3 To hide any columns in the middle of the screen, right-click on the column header and select Hide column

4 Click Print on the File ribbon to preview and print

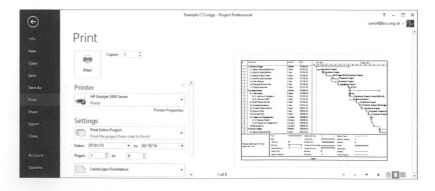

Page Setup and Scaling

In addition to Preview, Print on the File ribbon also gives you some options: number of copies, printer, settings, orientation and paper size. It also has a link to Page Setup, where you can change the margins, header, footer and various other options from the relevant tabs. One useful option for printed reports is scaling.

1 Select Print from the File ribbon and click the Page Setup link (underneath the Page Settings) to open the Page Setup dialog box, as illustrated below

2 Select the Page tab, then scale by changing the Adjust to: percentage or select Fit to: and specify the number of pages wide and tall, then click OK to see the revised print preview (as below)

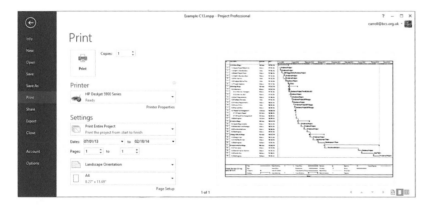

3 From the print preview, click the Page Setup link to return to the page setup dialog box to make further adjustments or click Print when you are happy

In the example above we have scaled the whole project to fit onto a single page by selecting Fit to: one page wide by one page tall.

By comparison, if we had clicked print from the preview screen on the page opposite the same report would have used eight pages to print.

Hot tip

Previewing reports is covered in more detail on page 164.

Reports

There are 20 predefined report formats available in Project 2013 together with new and custom groups, where you can create your own report formats, either based on an existing report format or starting from new with one of four blank reports.

1 Select one of the report groups (other than New Report) from the Project ribbon (as illustrated above) to open the drop down menu as illustrated right. This lists recently accessed reports together with More Reports

2 Click on More Reports to open the Reports dialog box as illustrated below

This lists the eight report groups down the left-hand side and the available reports for the selected group on the right-hand side.

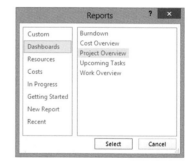

3 Click on the required report (such as Project Overview) and click Select to open the report preview as illustrated below

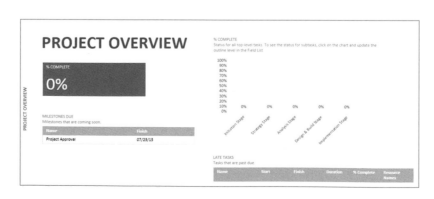

Report Templates & OfficeArt

Project 2013 has introduced some much improved project report templates together with support for OfficeArt. This allows you to create dynamic reports including pictures, tables, charts, shapes and even animations and hyperlinks, without the need to export data to other applications.

1 Select the report or template you wish to use (as explained opposite) for this example we have selected Work Overview from the Project Dashboard tab

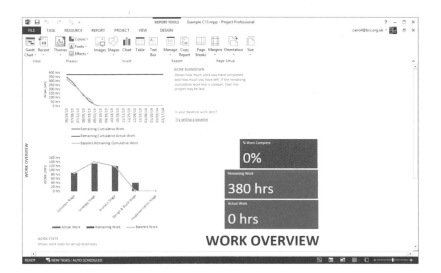

2 Now select images, shapes, charts or tables from the Design ribbon to add additional information to the report and delete or move other items as required

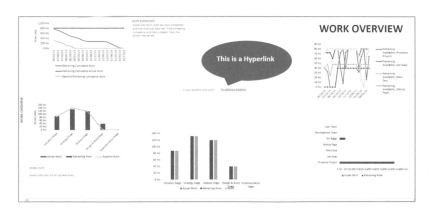

Previewing Reports

With Project, it is always a good idea to preview a report before printing it. That way you can make sure it will look the way you want it to and let you make any final adjustments to it. It may also save you wasting a lot of paper.

1 Open your project file in Gantt Chart view, Show all subtasks and zoom in to days within weeks view

2 Select Print on the File ribbon to open the Print and Print Preview screen, as illustrated below

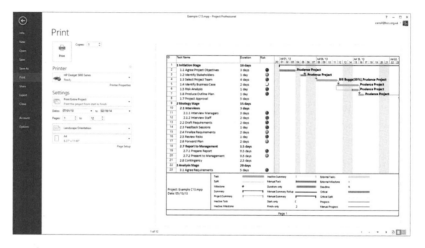

3 You can zoom the view in and out by clicking with your cursor (magnifying glass symbol) over the preview page on the right

4 Click the Multiple Pages button (bottom right-hand corner of the screen) to show the complete printout as illustrated below (printing Gantt charts over multiple pages can result in a lot of pages with no information on)

Hot tip

Viewing multiple pages can save you from wasting a lot of paper.

Visual Reports

Visual reports allows you to view your project data in Pivot Table reports in Microsoft Office Excel or Pivot Diagram views in Microsoft Office Visio Professional. There are several Excel and Visio templates provided with Project. These can also be edited, or you can create your own templates. As an example, we will create a budget cost report from a template for display in Excel.

1 In Gantt Chart view, select Visual Reports from the Project ribbon to open the Visual Report Create Report dialog box, as illustrated below right

2 To limit the number of templates displayed, check or uncheck the Excel and Visio check boxes at the top and select the category of report from the other six Category tabs (All is currently selected right)

3 Select the report template you wish to use (e.g. Budget Cost Report), click Edit Template to add or remove any required fields, then click View to display the report in the target application (the illustration below is an example of a budget cost report in an Excel Pivot Table)

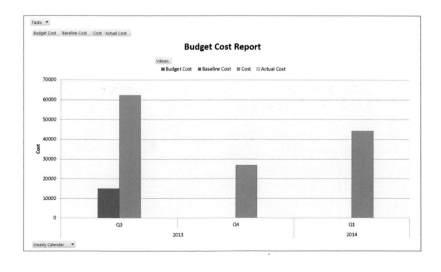

Copy Picture

Don't forget

If you wish to add Copy Picture to the Quick Access Toolbar, it's covered on page 32.

The Copy Picture facility in Project is useful for including information, such as Gantt charts, in project reports. It can be selected from the down arrow next to Copy on the Task ribbon (Clipboard group) or from the Quick Access Toolbar.

1 First format your screen to show the information you require (in this example we are focusing on the work scheduled for the next few weeks)

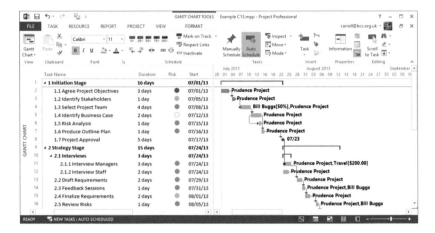

2 Select Copy > Copy Picture from the Task ribbon to open the Copy Picture dialog box

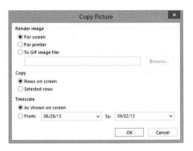

3 Select Render image for screen or printer, as required, adjust the timescale, if required, and click OK

4 Open your target Office application (Word in this example) and paste the picture into the document in the required position, as illustrated right

Copy Report

Similar to the Copy Picture facility, the Copy Report facility allows you to copy content from reports.

1 Select the report you wish to copy (as covered on page 162). For the following example we have selected a Burndown diagram (a new features in Project 2013)

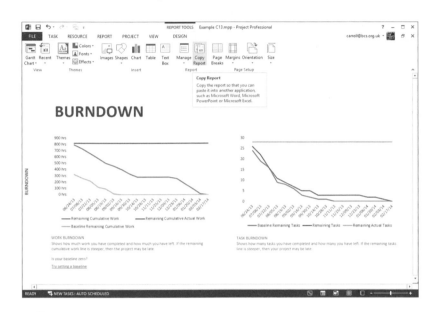

Hot tip

Burndown diagram was explained on page 10.

2 Click on Copy Report on the Design ribbon (this is displayed automatically when you select a report) as illustrated above

3 Open your target application (in this case PowerPoint) and paste the image (as illustrated below)

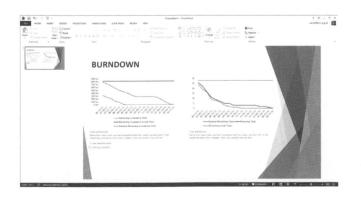

Enhanced Copy/Paste

The Copy and Paste features now retain Project's outline levels and formatting information for sharing information between Project and other Office applications.

1 In Gantt Chart view, select Timeline from the View ribbon to display the timeline in a split window

2 Select Copy Timeline (for email, presentation or full-size) from the Format ribbon, enter your target application and paste with format (to be able to adjust the pasted item), as illustrated in PowerPoint below

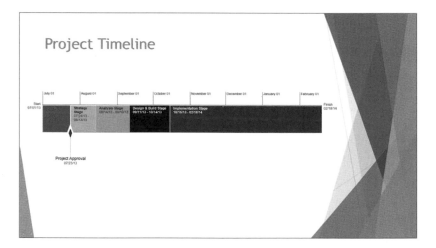

3 Once pasted into the target application, the whole image can be moved and re-sized in the normal way and each individual element of the image can also be edited

In a similar way, the timeline can be copied and pasted into Outlook and other office applications. Besides the timeline, any other elements of Project views can be copied and pasted.

...cont'd

As a further example, we will look at copying and pasting a task list from Project into Outlook.

1 In Gantt Chart view, select the columns and rows you wish to copy (as illustrated below) and click Copy on the Task ribbon (Clipboard group)

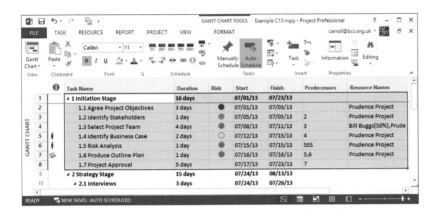

2 Open your target application (Outlook in this example), create a new email message and paste with format

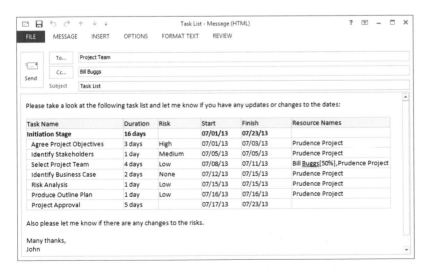

Please take a look at the following task list and let me know if you have any updates or changes to the dates:

Task Name	Duration	Risk	Start	Finish	Resource Names
Initiation Stage	**16 days**		**07/01/13**	**07/23/13**	
Agree Project Objectives	3 days	High	07/01/13	07/03/13	Prudence Project
Identify Stakeholders	1 day	Medium	07/05/13	07/05/13	Prudence Project
Select Project Team	4 days	Low	07/08/13	07/11/13	Bill Buggs[50%],Prudence Project
Identify Business Case	2 days	None	07/12/13	07/15/13	Prudence Project
Risk Analysis	1 day	Low	07/15/13	07/15/13	Prudence Project
Produce Outline Plan	1 day	Low	07/16/13	07/16/13	Prudence Project
Project Approval	5 days		07/17/13	07/23/13	

Also please let me know if there are any changes to the risks.

Many thanks,
John

3 The pasted object can be positioned and re-sized, as required, and edited as a table (in the example illustrated above, the Predecessors column has been deleted and some of the column sizes have been adjusted for best view)

Share

As part of the backstage overhaul, there are now two tabs on the File menu replacing Project Collaboration: Share and Export. Share gives two options for sharing project information:

Save and Sync

The first option is to Synchronize with a SharePoint Task List:

1 Select the File tab and Share to open the Share screen (as illustrated below)

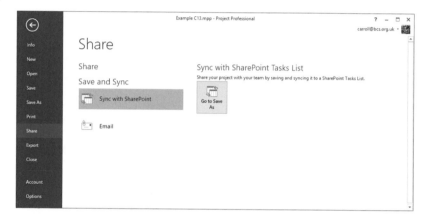

2 Select Sync with SharePoint and click on the "Go to Save As" icon (as illustrated above)

3 Select the Place (on the left) and Browse (on the right) to select the location of the Task List and click Save

Share

The second option is to share by email:

4 Select Share > Email and click on "Send As Attachment" to open your email program with the project file attached

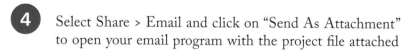

Export

The second new tab on the File menu, Export, provides options for exporting project files to other formats and to other versions of Project:

Create PDF/XPS Document

PDF and XPS formats provide a way of communicating project information to people who do not have access to Microsoft Project. Free viewers are widely available for both and both preserve the formatting and images.

1 Click on Create PDF/XPS, select the required file type, name and location for the file and click on OK to open the Document Export Options dialog box

2 Select the required formatting options and click on OK to create the export file

Save as Project File

This option (as illustrated on the right) allows you to export your project file to earlier versions of Project, to a Project template, Excel workbook or XML file. It also has a Save As option allowing other formats to be specified.

Summary

- Any chart or table view can be printed using the print function on the File ribbon, but it is worth spending a little time formatting the printout first

- Page setup can be used in Project in the normal way, to control the format (orientation, paper size, margins and legends) of a report

- Scaling can be used to reduce the number of pages that will be printed or to ensure that all the required information appears together on the same page

- In addition to being able to print from any view, there are 20 predefined reports and four new report formats that can be printed and customized

- With improved report templates and OfficeArt it is simple to customize reports for maximum impact

- Before printing anything from Project, it is a very good idea to use print preview. Then the format and layout can be checked (and changed where necessary) before printing. It can also help to prevent wasting paper, as Project can generate quite a lot of empty or nearly empty pages

- Visual reports allows data to be passed in a seamless manner between Project and Excel (as a pivot table) or Visio Professional (as a pivot diagram) for manipulation and display

- Copy Picture allows a snapshot of the screen to be taken (with some editing options) and Copy Report copies a complete report for pasting into other documents

- Enhanced copy and paste allows graphic and text data to be passed to other office applications with formatting and outline information retained

- Share facilities allow the sharing and synchronizing of task lists and project files through SharePoint and by email

- Export provide a range of options for sharing project information to earlier versions of Project, to templates, as PDF or XML documents and to other formats and mediums

14 Tracking Progress

Once the project is underway, you need to update it with details of progress. This chapter covers the different types of progress information and how to deal with them.

Progress Tracking

Hot tip

Set a baseline (see page 124) before you start tracking progress and updating your project data.

Once you have created your project plan and schedule, and the project has started, you can start tracking actual progress against the plan. You can enter information about progress on tasks by using actual start and finish dates, you can also input progress information on the percentage completed, actual and remaining duration, actual and remaining work, and actual and remaining cost. The most accurate way of tracking progress is by recording the actual work done and estimated work to completion on each task. However, it is also the most time consuming so many people use the simpler percentage completed.

Depending on the type of information you input, Project will calculate the other relevant information. If you input a task finish date, Project will set the actual start date to the scheduled start date, and the actual duration to the difference between the start date and actual completion date.

Before you begin to enter actual information, complete your plan in as much detail as you are able, using contingency to allow for the unknown. Once you are happy with the plan, you can set a baseline and then start progress tracking.

Project stores information under three headings:

Baseline
The plan dates and task durations are stored when you set a baseline. These are then used to compare with the actual and scheduled dates.

Actual
Actual work that has taken place on tasks, which have been completed or part completed, and the date the work was started and completed.

Schedule
The planned dates and durations of tasks that have not yet been started or have been started but not yet completed.

As you enter your actual data, Project recalculates the schedule. So start with the earliest tasks on the schedule and work through. Once you have input all the actual information, and seen the impact on the schedule, you can re-evaluate the project and make any adjustments required to the project tasks to deal with any issues that have arisen.

Completed Work

Once a task has been completed, the easiest way to enter that
information is by simply telling Project that the task is completed.

1 In Gantt Chart view, click to select the completed task

2 Click the down arrow next to Mark On Track on the
Task ribbon and select Update Tasks to open the Update
Tasks dialog box, as illustrated below

3 Click the Actual
Finish down arrow,
select the finish date
and click OK

4 If you open the
Update Tasks dialog
box again, you will
see that the actual
start date has also
been set, the task
is 100% complete
and the remaining
duration is now zero

5 Note also that a dark-blue progress line has been drawn
through the task and a tick has been placed in the task's
information box (both indicating that the task has now
been completed)

	ℹ	Task Name	Duration	Start	Finish	Jul 01, '13 30 01 02 03 04 05 06
1		⊿ 1 Initiation Stage	16 days	07/01/13	07/23/13	
2	✓	1.1 Agree Project Objectives	1 day	07/01/13	07/01/13	Prudence Project
3		1.2 Identify Stakeholders	1 day	07/05/13	07/05/13	Pr

6 Position your cursor over the Task Information box to
display the date completed, as illustrated below

1		⊿ 1 Initiation Stage	16 days	07/01/13	07/23/13	
2	✓	1.1 Agree Project Objectives	1 day	07/01/13	07/01/13	Prudence Project
3		This task was completed on 07/01/13.	1 day	07/05/13	07/05/13	Pr
4		1.3 Select Project Team	4 days	07/08/13	07/11/13	
5	⫯	1.4 Identify Business Case	2 days	07/12/13	07/15/13	

Part Completed Work

Where a number of days or hours of work have been carried out on a task, but the task is not yet fully completed, you can enter the actual work carried out.

1 In Task Usage view, select Work Table from the View ribbon and select Work (planned) and Actual Work (carried out) from the Format ribbon

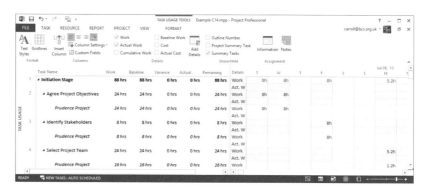

2 Click in the Actual Work field of the resource for which you wish to enter the details, type the number of hours of actual work and press Enter

Task Name	Work	Baseline	Variance	Actual	Remaining	Details	W	T	F	S
2 ◢ Agree Project Objectives	8 hrs	24 hrs	-16 hrs	8 hrs	0 hrs	Work				
						Act. W				
Prudence Project	8 hrs	24 hrs	-16 hrs	8 hrs	0 hrs	Work				
						Act. W				
3 ◢ Identify Stakeholders	8 hrs	8 hrs	0 hrs	5 hrs	3 hrs	Work	5h		3h	
						Act. W	5h			
Prudence Project	8 hrs	8 hrs	0 hrs	5 hrs	3 hrs	Work	5h		3h	
						Act. W	5h			
4 ◢ Select Project Team	24 hrs	24 hrs	0 hrs	0 hrs	24 hrs	Work				
						Act. W				

Note that the actual hours (5 hours in the above example) are rolled-up for the task. The work for the day is reduced to 5 hours and the remaining work (3 hours) is now scheduled on the next working day. Project assumes that the time you have entered is "as at" the end of the day and carries forward any remaining work.

3 If the remaining work is now expected to take longer than the original estimate (3 hours in the example above), this can be entered by selecting the carried forward work field for the following day and entering whatever the new estimate to completion is

Hot tip

Actual work to date + estimate to completion is the most accurate way of tracking progress.

Percentage Completed

There is a certain amount of risk involved in using percentage completed as the measure of work done on a task. It is human nature for most people to be optimistic about their progress, so actual work to date plus estimated work to completion is usually more accurate. However, it will sometimes be appropriate to use percentage completed, where it is not practical to track work in a more detailed way.

1 Open your project in Task Sheet view, click Tables on the View ribbon and select Tracking from the drop down list

	Task Name	Act. Start	Act. Finish	% Comp.	Phys. % Comp.	Act. Dur.	Rem. Dur.	Act. Cost	Act. Work
1	⊿ 1 Initiation Stage	NA	NA	0%	0%	0 days	16 days	$520.00	0 hrs
2	1.1 Agree Project Objectives	07/01/13	07/01/13	100%	0%	1 day	0 days	$320.00	8 hrs
3	1.2 Identify Stakeholders	07/03/13	NA	0%	0%	0 days	1 day	$200.00	5 hrs
4	1.3 Select Project Team	NA	NA	0%	0%	0 days	4 days	$0.00	0 hrs
5	1.4 Identify Business Case	NA	NA	0%	0%	0 days	2 days	$0.00	0 hrs
6	1.5 Risk Analysis	NA	NA	0%	0%	0 days	1 day	$0.00	0 hrs
7	1.6 Produce Outline Plan	NA	NA	0%	0%	0 days	1 day	$0.00	0 hrs

Hot tip

Note that the 5 hours work entered opposite is recorded but no % Comp has been calculated.

2 Update the percentage completed for tasks using the 25%, 50%, 75% functions on the Task ribbon (as illustrated right), if appropriate, or use the Update Tasks function (from Mark on Track) to input any other percentages

3 Select Gantt Chart from the Task ribbon to switch back to Gantt Chart view and note that the part completed tasks will have partial completion bars through them, as illustrated in the example below

	❶	Task Name	Duration	Start	Finish	Jul 01, '13 ... Jul 08, '13
1		⊿ 1 Initiation Stage	16 days	07/01/13	07/23/13	
2	✓	1.1 Agree Project Objectives	1 day	07/01/13	07/01/13	Prudence Project
3		1.2 Identify Stakeholders	1 day	07/03/13	07/05/13	Prudence Project
4		1.3 Select Project Team	4 days	07/08/13	07/11/13	Bill B
5		1.4 Identify Business Case	2 days	07/12/13	07/15/13	
6		1.5 Risk Analysis	1 day	07/15/13	07/15/13	
7		1.6 Produce Outline Plan	1 day	07/16/13	07/16/13	
8		1.7 Project Approval	5 days	07/17/13	07/23/13	

In this example we have input 65% completion on task 1.2 (using Update Tasks) and 50% on task 1.3 (using the 50% button). This can all be done directly in Gantt Chart view.

Duration Completed

You can enter the actual and remaining duration for a task in a similar way to the way you can enter actual work done.

1 In Gantt Chart view, select the task you want to enter duration information for

2 Select Update Tasks (from Mark on Track) on the Tasks ribbon to open the Update Tasks dialog box

3 Type in the actual duration to date, the remaining duration and click OK to update the task

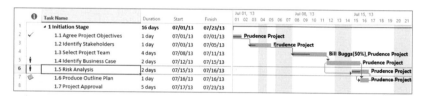

4 Select Update Tasks again and note that Percentage complete and Actual Start date have now been updated in line with the actual and remaining duration

As well as updating duration, the Update Tasks dialog box can also be used to update the percentage completed and the actual start and finish dates. Changes made to any of these fields will result in Project updating the other fields as appropriate, to keep the task details correct.

In the same way, the actual and remaining duration can also be edited directly in the Task Sheet Tracking view, as used in the Percentage Completed topic on the previous page. There are often several ways of doing the same thing in Project.

Entering Costs

Project will normally calculate costs for you based on the actual work involved in the task, and the cost details you entered for the resource assigned to the task. However, you can also enter actual cost details directly.

1 Select Options from the File menu, Schedule from the options list and scroll right down to the Calculation options

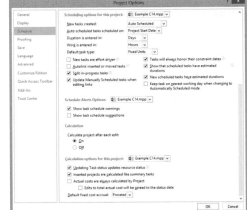

2 Clear the "Actual costs are always calculated by Project" check box and click OK

3 In Task Usage view, click Tables on the View ribbon and select Tracking from the drop down list

4 Select Cost and Actual Cost on the Format ribbon and de-select Work or any other details selected

5 Now select the Actual Cost field for the relevant task and resource and enter the actual cost (as illustrated below)

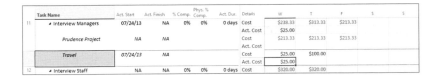

	Task Name	Act. Start	Act. Finish	% Comp.	Phys. % Comp.	Act. Dur.	Details	W	T	F	S	S
11	▲ Interview Managers	07/24/13	NA	0%	0%	0 days	Cost	$238.33	$313.33	$213.33		
							Act. Cost	$25.00				
	Prudence Project	NA	NA				Cost	$213.33	$213.33	$213.33		
							Act. Cost					
	Travel	07/24/13	NA				Cost	$25.00	$100.00			
							Act. Cost	$25.00				
12	▲ Interview Staff	NA	NA	0%	0%	0 days	Cost	$320.00	$320.00			

While it is possible to enter all resource costs in this manner, it would become fairly time consuming. On the whole, it is far simpler to let Project calculate resource costs for you as you can vary the rate for different types of work (as covered in Variable Resource Costs, Cost Rate Tables and Applying Resource Rates in Chapter 8).

Updating as Scheduled

If you have one or more tasks that have been started and/or completed in line with your schedule, you can use the Mark on Track function on the Task ribbon or Update Project dialog box from the Project ribbon.

1 In Gantt Chart view, select Update Project from the Project ribbon

2 Select "Update work as complete through", select the date you want all tasks updated to and click OK

3 If you receive a Planning Wizard warning that some unstarted tasks could not be rescheduled, click OK to continue, and update the Gantt chart (you can check the constraints on the relevant tasks later)

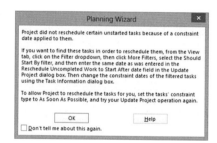

In the example above, the Gantt chart shows tasks 1.1 to 1.5 as fully complete and task 1.6 partially complete.

As can be seen in the Update Tasks dialog box (above right), the task actually started on the day selected at Step 2 (above). It is currently 50% complete and it is scheduled to be completed at the end of the next working day.

Actual v Baseline

Having set the project baseline, you can monitor your actual progress against this baseline at any time. The baseline and actual figures can be displayed in a number of tables and through the use of Tracking Gantt Chart view.

As an example, we will increase the actual work on a task and view the results.

1 In Gantt Chart view, select a task and use Update Task to increase the remaining duration (in this case to 2 days)

2 Click Tables on the View ribbon and select Work from the drop down list to open the Work Table

	Task Name	Work	Baseline	Variance	Actual	Remaining	% W. Comp.
2	1.1 Agree Project Objective	8 hrs	24 hrs	-16 hrs	8 hrs	0 hrs	100%
3	1.2 Identify Stakeholders	8 hrs	8 hrs	0 hrs	8 hrs	0 hrs	100%
4	1.3 Select Project Team	24 hrs	24 hrs	0 hrs	24 hrs	0 hrs	100%
5	1.4 Identify Business Case	16 hrs	16 hrs	0 hrs	16 hrs	0 hrs	100%
6	1.5 Risk Analysis	16 hrs	8 hrs	8 hrs	16 hrs	0 hrs	100%
7	1.6 Produce Outline Plan	24 hrs	8 hrs	16 hrs	8 hrs	16 hrs	33%
8	1.7 Project Approval	0 hrs	0 hrs	0 hrs	0 hrs	0 hrs	0%

Hot tip

You can use the Filter on the Variance column to display non-zero values.

Note in Table View that Work = Actual + Remaining and that Variance = Work - Baseline.

Note also that, in the example above, we have used background cell highlighting (see page 155) to highlight the variances (this is not an automatic feature of Project).

3 Select the Cost table to display the actual and baseline cost and Variance table (as below) to see the start and finish date variance (highlighted below)

	Task Name	Start	Finish	Baseline Start	Baseline Finish	Start Var.	Finish Var.
1	◢ 1 Initiation Stage	07/01/13	07/23/13	07/01/13	07/23/13	0 days	0 days
2	1.1 Agree Project Objectives	07/01/13	07/01/13	07/01/13	07/03/13	0 days	-2 days
3	1.2 Identify Stakeholders	07/03/13	07/05/13	07/05/13	07/05/13	-1 day	-0.63 days
4	1.3 Select Project Team	07/08/13	07/11/13	07/08/13	07/11/13	0 days	0 days
5	1.4 Identify Business Case	07/12/13	07/15/13	07/12/13	07/15/13	0 days	0 days
6	1.5 Risk Analysis	07/15/13	07/16/13	07/15/13	07/15/13	0 days	1 day
7	1.6 Produce Outline Plan	07/17/13	07/19/13	07/16/13	07/16/13	1 day	3 days

Tracking Gantt Chart

The Tracking Gantt Chart view gives a graphical representation of the actual state of the project compared to the baseline.

 1 In Gantt Chart view, select Tracking Gantt from the drop down list of Views on the Task ribbon

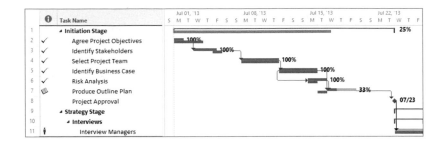

Note that in the example above:

● Percentage completed is displayed to the right of task bars and summary task bars

● The baseline task bars are displayed in gray below the actual and schedule task bars

● Outline numbering does not appear in Tracking Gantt Chart view

● Completed tasks (actual work) are displayed with dark blue task bars

● Scheduled tasks (not yet started) are displayed with light red (if on the critical path) or light blue (if not) task bars

● Started but not completed tasks are displayed with red (if on the critical path) or blue (if not) part dark, part light task bars

● Milestones are displayed as black diamonds, baseline milestones are displayed as black and white diamonds

Building in some lag time allows you to cope with task delays without ruining the schedule.

From the tracking Gantt chart above, we can see that, despite some variances, the project is currently on schedule for the first milestone (note: the baseline milestone is not actually visible above as it is hidden underneath the project milestone). There is also a five day lag time between Producing the Outline Project Plan and Project Approval which could be reduced if necessary.

Budget Tracking

Project has some good facilities for cost and budget tracking. The Cost resource type allows costs to be allocated for travel and expenses, in addition to resource costs and fixed costs. Budgets can also be assigned at the stage-level (summary task) or at the project-level and tracked in more detail.

1 To review total costs for tasks, select Task Sheet view from the drop down list on the Task ribbon

2 Click Tables on the View ribbon and select Cost from the drop down list to display the total cost fields

	Task Name	Fixed Cost	Fixed Cost Accrual	Total Cost	Baseline	Variance	Actual	Remaining
1	▲ 1 Initiation Stage	$0.00	Prorated	$3,920.00	$3,600.00	$320.00	$3,280.00	$640.00
2	1.1 Agree Project Objectives	$0.00	Prorated	$320.00	$960.00	($640.00)	$320.00	$0.00
3	1.2 Identify Stakeholders	$0.00	Prorated	$320.00	$320.00	$0.00	$320.00	$0.00
4	1.3 Select Project Team	$0.00	Prorated	$1,040.00	$1,040.00	$0.00	$1,040.00	$0.00
5	1.4 Identify Business Case	$0.00	Prorated	$640.00	$640.00	$0.00	$640.00	$0.00
6	1.5 Risk Analysis	$0.00	Prorated	$640.00	$320.00	$320.00	$640.00	$0.00
7	1.6 Produce Outline Plan	$0.00	Prorated	$960.00	$320.00	$640.00	$320.00	$640.00

3 To review costs by resource, select Resource Sheet view, click Tables on the View ribbon and select Cost, then select Group By Resource Type on the View ribbon

	Resource Name	Cost	Baseline Cost	Variance	Actual Cost	Remaining	Add New Column
	▲ Type: Work	$123,424.00	$123,104.00	$320.00	$3,280.00	$120,144.00	
1	Prudence Project	$21,344.00	$21,024.00	$320.00	$2,880.00	$18,464.00	
2	Joe Soap	$0.00	$0.00	$0.00	$0.00	$0.00	
3	Mary Dee	$0.00	$0.00	$0.00	$0.00	$0.00	
4	Wendy Page	$0.00	$0.00	$0.00	$0.00	$0.00	
5	Bill Buggs	$2,080.00	$2,080.00	$0.00	$400.00	$1,680.00	
11	Development Team	$60,000.00	$60,000.00	$0.00	$0.00	$60,000.00	
12	User Team	$40,000.00	$40,000.00	$0.00	$0.00	$40,000.00	
	▲ Type: Material	$0.00	$0.00	$0.00	$0.00	$0.00	
6	Paint	$0.00	$0.00	$0.00	$0.00	$0.00	
7	Carpet	$0.00	$0.00	$0.00	$0.00	$0.00	
	▲ Type: Cost	$125.00	$200.00	($75.00)	$25.00	$100.00	
8	Travel	$125.00	$200.00	($75.00)	$25.00	$100.00	

4 To review stage costs, select Task Sheet view and Show Outline Level 1 as illustrated below

	Task Name	Fixed Cost	Fixed Cost Accrual	Total Cost	Baseline	Variance	Actual	Remaining
0	▲ Example C14	$0.00	Prorated	$133,549.00	$26,264.00	$107,285.00	$3,305.00	$130,244.00
1	▷ 1 Initiation Stage	$0.00	Prorated	$3,920.00	$3,600.00	$320.00	$3,280.00	$640.00
9	▷ 2 Strategy Stage	$0.00	Prorated	$5,965.00	$6,040.00	($75.00)	$25.00	$5,940.00
22	▷ 3 Analysis Stage	$0.00	Prorated	$14,864.00	$14,864.00	$0.00	$0.00	$14,864.00
27	▷ 4 Design & Build Stage	$0.00	Prorated	$61,760.00	$61,760.00	$0.00	$0.00	$61,760.00
31	▷ 5 Implementation Stage	$0.00	Prorated	$47,040.00	$47,040.00	$0.00	$0.00	$47,040.00

Hot tip

To add the project total (as illustrated) select Project Summary Task from the Format ribbon.

Project Statistics

The Project Statistics dialog box gives summary-level information for the whole project.

1 Select Project Information from the Project ribbon to open the Project Information dialog box

2 Click the Statistics button to open the Project Statistics dialog box (as illustrated below)

	Start	Finish
Current	07/01/13	02/18/14
Baseline	07/01/13	02/18/14
Actual	07/01/13	NA
Variance	0d	0d

	Duration	Work	Cost
Current	164d	804h	$133,549.00
Baseline	164d	380h	$26,264.00
Actual	5.52d	24.55h	$3,305.00
Remaining	158.48d	779.45h	$130,244.00

Percent complete:

Duration: 3%   Work: 3%

Project Statistics for 'Example C14.mpp'

Close

Top Section
The top section of the Project Statistics dialog box shows the Current, Baseline and Actual Project Start and Finish Dates, together with the number of days Variance.

Middle Section
The middle section shows a summary of the Current, Baseline, Actual and Remaining Duration, Work and Cost. In the example above, duration, work and cost have all increased since the baseline was first set.

Bottom Section
Finally, the Percentage complete by Duration and Work is shown.

These project statistics are useful for a high-level snapshot report on the current status of the project.

Progress Lines

Progress Lines can be drawn on the Gantt Chart or Tracking Gantt Chart views at any date, to show the actual or expected progress as at that date.

They work by linking the tasks that are scheduled to be started, in progress or completed on that date. Tasks that are behind schedule result in peaks to the left of the line, while tasks that are ahead of schedule result in peaks to the right of the line.

1 In Gantt Chart or Tracking Gantt Chart view, click Gridlines on the Format ribbon and select Progress Lines from the drop down list

2 Under "Current progress line" select Display (top left), "Display progress in relation to" Baseline

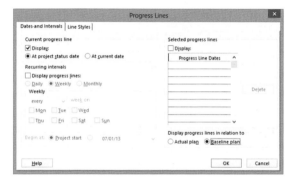

plan (bottom right), and then click OK to show the progress line, as illustrated in the example below

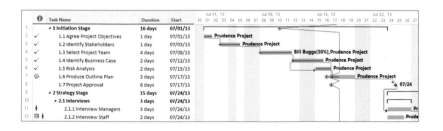

In the example above, the progress line (in red) has been shown as at the end of day on Wednesday, July 17 (the current status date). At that date one task (Produce Outline Project Plan) was originally scheduled to be completed, but is not yet completed. On the Initiation Stage summary bar (at the top of the chart), the progress line is indicating that the stage is five days behind the original baseline schedule.

Summary

- Once you have scheduled your project and allocated resources, you need to start tracking the actual progress of work on tasks against schedule

- If a task has been fully completed, you can mark it as completed by simply entering the finish date into the Update Tasks dialog box

- If a task is only part completed, work can be input as hours actually worked and estimated hours remaining to completion in Task Usage view

- The simplest way of inputting part completed work is to set the percentage complete in Task Sheet view, or use the percentage functions on the Task ribbon, but this is a less accurate method of tracking progress

- Duration completed and remaining duration can be input using the Update Tasks dialog box

- Actual costs of work completed can be entered in Task Usage view, but it is generally easier to allow Project to calculate the cost of work from the resource information

- Updating as scheduled is a quick way of entering progress information, if tasks are being completed more or less on schedule

- Having set a baseline, actual progress can be compared to baseline using the Work, Cost and Variance tables in Gantt Chart view

- Tracking Gantt Chart view gives you a view of actual and scheduled tasks superimposed over the baseline

- Budget tracking can be done by task or resource by applying the Cost table and, in summary, for stages and the complete project by showing the project summary task

- Project statistics gives you a summary view of current project progress against the baseline

- Finally, progress lines can add a visual indication of the state of the project at any point in time

Index